LANCE: A Spirit Unbroken
Walter Stoffel

To Susie(sic),
Remember to "Paws"
to enjoy Life!
Walter Stoffel

PUBLISHED BY

DIAMOND PUBLISHING INTERNATIONAL

DIAMOND PUBLISHING INTERNATIONAL

Lance: A Spirit Unbroken
ISBN-13 978-0-9861500-0-5
ISBN-13 978-0-9861500-2-9

PRINTED IN THE U.S.A.

Published by Diamond Publishing International
148 Sportsmen Drive
Canadensis, Pa. 18326
570-994-3627
www.diamondpublishinginternational.com
Contact the author: walterstoffelauthor@gmail.com

Front and back cover design by Caryn Newton and Lynn Snipes.
Photo on page 22 © Cynoclub/Dreamstime.com.
Author's publicity photo by Nikki DePaul of 27RosePhotography.
All other photos by author or his wife.

I wrote this book to honor Lance, a never-to-be-duplicated, hard-luck dog with an unbreakable spirit. Trapped from birth in a web of violence, Lance's desperate decade-long struggle to stay alive demands to be heard. Though nothing can make up for the endless string of assaults he suffered, this book is my attempt to at least bring Lance out of the painful obscurity he lived in for so long and give him the recognition he deserves.

It would be a huge mistake to view Lance as a typical abused dog (is there such an animal?) or a typical anything else, for that matter. If using one word to describe Lance, I'd pick unique. Unique because he should have been dead long before I ever met him. Unique because, despite all he had been through, his keen intellect and quirky personality could still impress, amaze, and amuse. Unique because Lance was a teacher who inspired me to reexamine the meaning of life in general, and mine in particular. Hopefully, you will find that uniqueness woven into the pages of this book.

My experience with Lance showed me just how easily animal abuse can go undetected and ignored, and I'm hoping Lance's story will open others' eyes to this sad fact. If this book makes one dog's life safer, then my writing will not have been in vain.

No doubt my shortcomings as a dog rescuer and owner are on full display in this book. Perhaps there are lessons to be learned from any lapses in good judgement I may have had before and after rescuing Lance.

As an accomplished procrastinator, I have often started numerous projects that were never completed. This one was, thanks to the "hounding" of a very special dog. So, please read, enjoy, and, as I did, learn from Lance.

Dedication

This book is dedicated to Lance, who provided the material and inspiration, and to every other dog (and cat, for that matter) that ever got a raw deal. This book is also dedicated to my loved and loving wife Clara, who patiently endured Lance's orneriness and my recklessness.

Acknowledgements

For serving as my muse and providing invaluable assistance throughout the work of chronicling Lance's life, I owe a huge debt to all the members of Barbara's Writing Group based in Stroudsburg, Pennsylvania. I also extend thanks to Oli Landwijt and Professor Meghann Ryan for their editing services and to Mary Shafer of IndieNavigator.com, whose consulting advice was invaluable throughout the process of making this book a reality.

Caryn Newton of Lantern Glow Design skillfully constructed the interior and exterior book designs. Lynn Tarrant Snipes created the original cover artwork. The author's photograph was provided by Nikki DePaul of 27Rose Photography. Jillian Baker and Vicki Ayala provided their computer expertise to bring Lance to life on the Internet.

Last, but not least, I am immensely grateful to my late sister Liz, whose generosity played a vital part in Lance's rescue.

Disclaimer

Certain names in this book have been changed for the purposes of maintaining confidentiality. Any resemblance between those names and any persons living or dead is purely coincidental.

Contents

-1-

Chance Meeting

"Do you want to adopt a dog?"

Turning my attention towards the voice, I saw a tall, slender, white-haired woman walking a leashed dog. Or rather, I saw a dog pulling a leashed woman. The dog, a black-and-white, medium-sized ball of fire, yanked her in whatever direction happened to strike his fancy while she struggled to keep her balance.

"Not really. Anyway, if I did, it'd be the one up the street. You know, the one that's stuck outside all the time."

When I was new to the area and jogged by his property, the dog in question used to come charging at me, barking vociferously, restrained by a short cable attached to a run. After a few months, he began ignoring me. Although I felt sorry for him, I was never sure if his brief interest in me had been friendly or unfriendly, and never tried to approach him. Years earlier, I had read somewhere that a dog kept outside 24/7 was not to be trusted.

"This *is* that dog!" announced the lady, all the while attempting to control her hyperactive companion. "My name is Anna and this is Lance."

Upon closer scrutiny (to the degree my 20/450 vision would allow), I realized that indeed he was. I was tempted to ask Anna why she kept her dog outside all the time, but before I could, she let me know Lance was technically not her dog. She explained that his legal owners, the Schmidts, had little interest in their dog and she'd taken it upon herself to care for him. That effort included walks like this day's that sorely tested her endurance. I had to get to work but, now knowing this dog was approachable, asked Anna if she thought his owners would object to my walking him on occasion. She assured me they wouldn't.

This accidental encounter occurred in front of my apartment on Boulder Drive in Mount Bethel, Pennsylvania, the first Tuesday in December 2001.

The following Saturday, after telling my wife Clara what I was up to, I walked over to the Schmidt residence. On the way, I wondered: *Do I really want to bother doing this? Yeah, I do, because I always felt bad for the poor pooch. People who neglect animals, what are they like? Did Anna tell them I might be stopping by? I hadn't bothered to check with her. What if they tell me to get lost? I guess that would be that. I tried.*

Arriving at the front stoop, I knocked on the screen door and waited. After a second and third series of knocks, the inside door opened up bringing me face-to-face with Mr. Schmidt. He was a light-complexioned, black-haired, forty-something man, around six feet tall, with a beer belly (I assumed beer was the cause based on the number of empties stacked along the side of the house). A conversation ensued through an unopened screen door.

"Hi, my name's Walter. I live down the street. I was wondering if I could walk your dog today."

"What for?"

"Well, I think I could give him a better workout than Anna can." I was quite sure of that, but I was just as sure that Mr. Schmidt could care less about how much exercise his dog got.

"It's up to you."

"I didn't bring a leash. Do you have one?"

"Jesus Christ, I guess so."

Without saying another word, he slammed the inside door shut and left me waiting on the stoop. Eventually, he returned holding a leash and stepped outside. We headed across the backyard.

While walking towards Lance's doghouse, a one-way conversation ensued, during which Mr. Schmidt endlessly ranted about the high cost of home heating oil. Did it seem odd to him that one more neighbor, one he didn't know at all, was taking an interest in his dog? I imagined him thinking *I'm talking with another idiot animal lover.*

Fortunately, the walk was brief, so I didn't have to endure his presence longer than necessary. There was simply an indefinable something about him that made me uncomfortable. I just wanted to get the dog and get out of there.

Once reaching Lance, Mr. Schmidt approached to leash him. His dog immediately sank to the ground and lay prone with his head scrunched between his two front legs, almost as if he was trying to hide his face. *Something seems odd, unnatural. Is that a bashful or meek expression? Can't tell.* I ultimately concluded he must be of a gentle and obedient nature. *Great, a dog that is rambunctious while exercising (Anna could attest to that!) and well-behaved when not.*

The second I took the leash from Mr. Schmidt, Lance came to life. Off we went on a chaotic tour of the neighborhood. Throughout, we engaged in a tug of war. Whatever he had seemed to be on the Schmidt property just minutes before was now out the window. This was the dog I'd seen running Anna ragged just a few days earlier. Completely unruly, he darted off in any direction that piqued his interest, pulling me with him. Every so often, while dragging me around the neighborhood, he stared back at the human holding the other end of the leash. He seemed to be evaluating me. Was I a friend or a foe? Could I be trusted? Our first walk lasted little more than twenty minutes but, for me at least, had felt like an hours-long wrestling match. What a whirlwind! When it was over, I returned Lance to his run, the leash to Mr. Schmidt, and headed back home, giving myself a mental pat on the back for a good deed done.

Before reaching my apartment I'd already made the decision to walk Lance again sometime soon. The problem? His owner. He creeped me out. I didn't want to deal with him on any kind of regular basis. With that in mind, I bought the sturdiest leash available at the local pet store, thus eliminating Mr. Schmidt as the middleman.

Funny. After several years of not having a dog, just a few minutes with this one instantly caught me up in his over-the-top enthusiasm. I felt like a kid again.

-2-

Outcast

A few days after that first walk, I called Anna to get more background information on Lance.

A Border Collie, he was born sometime in November of 1991. Apparently Joseph, Mr. Schmidt's father, had purchased him from a breeder (puppy mill?) to give to his grandsons as a Christmas present.

The Schmidts were a troubled family. For starters, Mr. Schmidt was an alcoholic, Mrs. Schmidt suffered from mental illness, and they both had recently taken out a PFA (protection from abuse order) against one of their sons. Joseph had hoped that a pet might bring them closer together.

After the holidays, Lance, only a few weeks old, had already been banished from the Schmidt house and was being kept outside, completely unsheltered, on a short, heavy, cumbersome chain. "The chain looked bigger than he was." Anna asked Mrs. Schmidt if Lance would ever be allowed back into her house. "No! He makes a mess and just gets in the way. He won't be coming into any house I own. I refuse to live in a sty!"

During the following weeks, Anna stopped by every day to check on the dog. The Schmidts hadn't bothered to name their dog and Anna soon tired of addressing him as "puppy," so she dubbed him Lance, after the brave medieval knight Sir Lancelot. Like his namesake, Lance would prove to be a staunch soldier.

A month after Lance had been evicted, Mount Bethel suffered a heavy snowstorm. Anna took a walk down to the Schmidt house during the blizzard. Her suspicions were confirmed. There sat Lance, motionless as a statue, still confined to the same spot. His face and torso were collecting snow, and small icicles were dangling from his shaggy, thick coat. Seeing Anna, he sprang to life and greeted her with a wagging tail. Not knowing what to do, she went back home. She phoned Papa Schmidt (Joseph) who told her he'd contacted the breeder/seller about returning the dog, but was told that "this is a business I'm running" and "done deals don't get undone." Lance's fate had been sealed.

A few days later, Anna again passed by the Schmidt residence. The temperature had gone up slightly above freezing, so Lance was no longer coated with icicles. Instead, he was soaking wet. Anna took action. She got permission from the Schmidts to provide Lance with a doghouse. Then she implored her husband Edward to build it and he agreed to. He brought the necessary building materials and tools to the Schmidt backyard and over the course of several weeks, in the dead of winter, constructed a solid wooden doghouse. Anna put some blankets and straw on the floor inside. After having survived completely exposed to winter's elements for well over a month, Lance was able to move into his new home. At the same time, Edward rigged up a run to which the dog was permanently attached. Joseph Schmidt agreed to continue feeding him. Throughout all this, the rest of the Schmidt family paid little attention. This puppy was simply not their concern. In Anna's words, "I doubt any of them ever petted Lance once."

Later that winter, Papa Schmidt died. Anna assumed that someone else in the Schmidt household would volunteer to feed the dog. She was wrong. Months went by and, apart from any occasional treats she had been bringing him, he was not getting any food. Anna admitted she wasn't the first person to realize this. One day she took a friend to see Lance. Upon seeing the dog, she turned to Anna and said, "This dog is not eating." Perhaps his thick coat had hidden his malnourished condition from Anna. Whatever the case, made aware of the situation, she took it upon herself to nourish him. She supplemented kibble with her own home cooking. Of course, food not immediately consumed was subject to the vagaries of the weather: freezing up in the winter, getting waterlogged in the rain, drawing flies and various other insects in warm weather, etc. Sometimes the food went rancid. His water bowl was subjected to bug infestation in warm weather and icing up in cold weather. During one heat wave, Anna suggested to Mrs. Schmidt that Lance needed more frequent changes of water, because it was quickly getting warm and bug-laden. Since he was on their property, she figured the Schmidts might more easily monitor his water supply. Mrs. Schmidt couldn't be bothered. "Haven't you heard? We're in a drought. That dog comes last."

If Anna went out of town she'd drop off dog food, hoping the Schmidts would feed Lance until she returned, but doubting they would.

That thought gnawed at her until she arrived back home. The first few days she resumed responsibility for feeding Lance, Anna noticed he ate "extra ravenously."

Anna found a veterinarian who was willing to treat Lance on the Schmidt's property as needed. When I asked her how often "as needed" occurred, she said that he "had his scrapes like any dog." I thought to myself, *Hey, he's on a run. How fair a fight is that? And with what was he fighting? Or whom?* One particularly violent confrontation with an unknown assailant had left him with an ear that was almost ripped completely off and needed to be sewn back together. Due to the severity of that particular wound, hospitalization was required. At Anna's insistence, the Schmidts reluctantly took Lance to an animal hospital. Mr. Schmidt made it clear his family wouldn't be imposed upon to do so in the future. "That mutt was the old man's idea, not ours."

When the visiting vet retired, Anna was unable to find another that made house calls. Over time, Lance's increasing unruliness and decreasing approachability made any type of medical care, on-site or otherwise, problematic. As a result, from age three on, if he suffered any medical problems, Lance was on his own.

Every so often, Anna arrived at the Schmidt property and found the dog tangled up in a combined web of bushes and the lead for his run, presumably after some skirmish. If she was away for a few days or even weeks, Lance might very well be left trapped, sometimes in a standing position, until she got back home. "Of course," Anna said, "I was the one who untangled him, not any of the Schmidts. I think they would have just left him that way for good."

Since his range of motion was restricted by the run, Lance's doghouse at times became surrounded by his own feces. Anna did all she could to keep his small living space clean, knowing no one else would.

As Lance got older, Anna realized he was living a totally sedentary life. She asked one of the two Schmidt boys, Ted, if it would be a problem if she gave the dog an occasional walk. He couldn't have cared less. He followed up "What for?" with "Do what you want." "I didn't bother to ask Mrs. Schmidt because she never gave me a straight answer about anything." Anna took on the additional task of exercising the dog to the extent she could. Unfortunately that meant this highly energetic canine got short walks once or twice a week "just around the neighborhood." Even these brief treks pushed Anna's stamina to its limits. She offered to pay some kids in the neighborhood to walk him, but found no takers. "I think Lance already had a bit of a reputation by that time."

Lance became painfully upset by thunder, firecrackers, and firearms. Anna took it upon herself to sit with Lance during Fourth of July celebrations in a futile attempt to comfort him, although nothing could be done to muffle the explosions. The rest of each year he had to handle loud noises on his own.

One winter, Anna tried to shelter Lance in her home during a severe ice storm. Proving himself way too unruly inside the house, she reluctantly had to take him back to his run to brave the frigid elements. She never attempted to house him again. During a subsequent winter, Anna went on vacation to Florida. When she returned, a local resident called to advise her that Lance, outside in a particularly bad blizzard, was heard yelping and whining nonstop. "My neighbor called and told me, 'The snow was higher than Lance was. He was trapped in his doghouse. He was crying. You should have heard him wailing.'" Indignant and frustrated, Anna lost it. "You bitch! Why didn't you do something about it instead of just waiting for me to come home so you could give me the bad news?"

The talk of cold weather and snow storms jarred my memory. I asked Anna about something that happened during a heavy snowfall just the previous winter. Clara and I had bundled up and taken a walk through the neighborhood. Along the way, we passed (what I now knew was) the Schmidt residence, complete with doghouse set in the backyard away from the house and the road. I told Clara that the dog there always seemed to be outside whenever I jogged by. This particular day there were no signs of life around the doghouse, which was already surrounded by well over a foot of snow. We both assumed the owners had let him inside due to the inclement weather. Had they? Anna was adamant. "Oh, no. No. He hasn't been back inside their house since he was a puppy. No way. Louise {Mrs. Schmidt} is a clean freak. She didn't like Lance from day one; she was angry at Papa Schmidt for buying him. She really doesn't like dogs, or cats, for that matter. None of them really do. If you didn't see him that day, I can guarantee you he was tucked inside his doghouse."

Were any assaults on Lance man-made? Anna said there was a rumor in the neighborhood that Mr. Schmidt had been seen taking a rake to the dog. When Anna asked him about it, he vehemently denied any such thing, demanding to know who had accused him. Not wanting to start a neighborhood war, Anna lied, telling him she wasn't sure.

According to Anna, another neighbor said she couldn't actually see what was happening on the Schmidt property from her house but, swore that one summer day she "heard it all, the wailing, that yelping and crying sound a dog makes when it's being hurt." She couldn't stand it so she "closed the windows, cranked up the air conditioner, and blasted the TV." Anna wasn't convinced. "I wouldn't believe her. She's always had a drinking problem…been to a couple of those hospitals, you know, the ones drunks go to. She's known to stir the pot with made-up stories."

However, Anna herself admitted that what interaction the Schmidts had with their dog "hasn't been too good." She caught Peter, one of the Schmidts' two sons, tormenting Lance by steering a seated power mower directly at him and around his doghouse after he had entered it for sanctuary. When she confronted him about it, he told her to "mind your own effin' business." She remembered that Ted, the other son, angry for having to drive Lance to the hospital when he suffered the torn ear, was "rough" getting him into a pickup truck.

There was another day when Anna arrived at the Schmidt property with a home-cooked meal for Lance. He didn't come out to greet her. No matter how hard she tried, she couldn't coax Lance out of his doghouse. It was not like him to refuse saying hello to her. She left his food and went back home. "I remember that Jack {Mr. Schmidt} was working in the garden right next to Lance's doghouse. I'm not really sure what was going on." The thought occurred to me that Lance's apparent meekness when being leashed a few days earlier might have had less to do with his inherent nature and more to do with having been near Mr. Schmidt.

On the one hand, Anna admitted she was reluctant to question any of the Schmidts about the way they treated Lance, because she feared that if she stuck up for the dog, he would pay the price when she wasn't around. On the other hand, she kept telling herself, and anyone that would listen, Lance's situation "wasn't as bad as it looked." The Schmidts were incompetent owners and she was compensating for their shortcomings—nothing more, nothing less. Maybe Anna had entered the land of denial. Sooner or later, most of us spend some time there.

Anna told me she knew there were some kids in the neighborhood that were, in her words, "not nice to Lance." She was reluctant to go into details, so that subject was dropped.

On numerous occasions, Lance showed up at Anna's place after breaking loose from his run. He was always taken back to the Schmidt property.

When friends and neighbors proposed stealing Lance, Anna talked them out of it. "I'm just not a lawbreaker."

During her years caring for Lance, Anna anonymously contacted local authorities on several occasions to see what recourse she had concerning the Schmidts and their refusal to care for Lance. She always got the same story. As long as a dog had some shelter and was being fed, he could legally be kept outside on a permanent basis. Anna had unintentionally boxed Lance into a catch-22 situation. The only way the Schmidts might be held accountable for neglecting Lance required removing the doghouse and food. If that were done, Anna was certain none of the Schmidts would lift a finger to help their dog. And who knew how long the bureaucracy would take before getting around to Lance's situation? In the meantime, he might starve or freeze to death. Further, if he survived and was subsequently removed from the Schmidt property, where would Lance go? Anna could not take him in. She had a dog and cat of her own and had already found out that Lance was not a house-friendly dog. Anna settled for the status quo: keeping him housed outside at the Schmidt place, while she continued to feed and walk him.

Except for her visits, Lance was alone, neglected, and at the mercy of nature, man, and other animals. As Anna put it, "Lance got lost," living as an exile right in his owners' backyard.

Despite this conversation a sad reality hadn't yet fully registered with me: Lance was doomed to spend the rest of his unnatural life just as he had for the last decade, alone and outside on the end of a run, waiting to die there.

**BORDER COLLIE PUPPY AT SAME AGE AS LANCE
WHEN HE WAS FORCED TO START LIVING OUTDOORS**

-3-

Pushing the Envelope

If the story Anna told me was all true, Lance had indeed been living a very grim life. But, was it all true? This dog had undoubtedly endured a hard life, but just how hard wasn't certain. I didn't know how much of Anna's story to believe. Lance had been stuck outside for at least a few years; I had witnessed that myself. Still, things didn't quite add up. Anna painted the picture of a dog that had been assaulted on numerous occasions by animals and, possibly, man. Such a dog would obviously look worse for wear. However, the dog I saw was a peppy, energetic ten-year-old spitfire. Something else didn't make sense. Why would Anna ask me to adopt a dog only to tell me days later that he had long ago become unapproachable for most people? To add to the mystery, on that first walk, I hadn't found him standoffish at all.

The whole setup was odd. If Anna was to be believed, the less contact any of the Schmidts had with Lance, the better. But that still left Lance stuck outside day and night. Since Anna had presumably been doing all the caretaking, why hadn't she simply taken Lance into her home? She had tried once. Why not give him a second chance? He certainly wasn't some feral beast. If not her, didn't she or the Schmidts have a family member or acquaintance who might have given him a shot at a home? Why hadn't someone in the neighborhood stepped up? If Anna's neighbors had supposedly wanted to steal Lance, why didn't one of them ever actually do it? Why would nobody want him?

How much of Anna's story was fact and not fiction? Not knowing her any better than I knew the Schmidts, I thought of getting their version about all this, but never did.

I *was* sure that Anna and the Schmidts had a strange relationship. Based on her story, the Schmidts were deadbeat parents. I guess that made Anna Lance's foster mother, even though he remained on the Schmidts' property. She's the one who had cared for him all these years, or so she said. Obviously, she was not up to the task of giving him the amount of exercise he needed, and no one else had volunteered for the job until now.

Apparently for Lance, whatever his life had been like, that was then and this was now. If he had indeed been living life on the wild side, he seemingly had come out of it unscathed. It was as if the previous ten years never happened. I think it was the philosopher Nietzsche who said that if something doesn't kill you, it makes you stronger. Lance was his proof.

Unruly? At times. Unapproachable? Maybe with some others, but he certainly wasn't with me. Outright dangerous? Not at all.

One thing was for sure: being stuck outside 24/7 was no way for a dog to live. Yet he seemed so happy-go-lucky. Anna's care must have offset the Schmidts' neglect. Whatever the case, his harsh lifestyle hadn't gotten the best of him. People could take a lesson from Lance on the art of survival. There was something unique about this dog.

His situation, while less than ideal, apparently was legal. That didn't make it right, however, there was nothing to do but make the best of it. Lance appeared healthy, had shelter (albeit only a doghouse), he was getting fed, and now all this dog needed was to finally get the exercise he had craved for so long. I became his entertainment committee. I looked forward to walking him, sort of a return to my youth (back then it was Rex, that great German Shepherd, my pal through thick and thin) and, being a bit of a fitness nut, this was also an opportunity to supplement my own workout regimen. Lance was clearly a spitfire, and would turn out to be a more than willing (and highly demanding) exercise partner.

We began to walk together on a regular basis. After that very first walk we'd taken, I no longer bothered to announce my presence to any of the Schmidts. I'd simply leash up Lance and off we'd go. After a few weeks of this, I often found him, having already sensed my impending arrival, standing as close to the edge of the road as his run would allow, ready to roll. He'd be wearing that bright-eyed *Oh boy! Let's get going!* look. Other times, if my arrival was unanticipated, I simply had to make a clucking sound with my tongue. Hearing this, Lance would ease out of his doghouse, hesitate briefly while determining who was visiting, and then, realizing it was I, yawn, do some stretching, and come charging up the sloping lawn to greet me. There was no longer any apparent reason to worry about his demeanor.

Before I could leash him, Lance always had to get a whole bunch of jumping up and down out of his system. The exuberant look on his face spoke volumes: *Thank you, oh thank you! Anna used to take me on walks but they were so short. The ones you and I go on are the kind I've dreamed about since I was a puppy. Thank you!*

Our walks became more frequent and lengthier. Lance had boundless energy. He continually pulled on the leash, going off into whatever direction appealed to him. He didn't seem to have any particular destination in mind; he simply wanted to be headed somewhere. Whenever I stopped to rest and offer Lance treats in an attempt to slow him down, he would have none of it. Instead, while tugging on his leash, he would first look off into the distance and then back at me as if he were saying: *Why stop? Let's keep going! There's so much to see!* Was he trying to make up for lost time?

Our journeys were aerobic workouts for me and an adventure for Lance. He had never before had so much exercise and, apparently, fun. They were more, for both of us. For me, these jaunts were also escapes from the stressors of adulthood: personal, job-related, and financial. I was a kid again, romping with a dog—not mine, but that didn't matter. As for Lance, the thought occurred to me that he wasn't reliving his childhood; he was living it for the first time.

It was bound to happen sooner or later. On one of our treks, we encountered a man and woman also out for a stroll, heading towards us from the opposite direction, on my right. As our paths crossed I said "Hello!" and began to pass by them. To my left, Lance was walking along the edge of the road sniffing this and that. Suddenly he crossed in front of me, made a mad dash at the woman, jumped up on her, sniffed her face and then, having lost interest, got down and came over to me after I gently tugged on the leash. Taken by surprise, she let out a startled "Oh!" I apologized and briskly walked on with Lance. He had passed his first test with other people—sort of.

I decided to measure the exact length of our treks utilizing my car's odometer. We were covering up to 6.9 miles per walk! That explained why I was so bushed following each jaunt. Yet, for Lance, it seemed that these were all mere warm-ups.

After weeks of hiking him on paved roads, I upped the stakes. I was getting walked to death by a leashed whirling dervish. If I could let Lance loose, he would be able to cover lots of distance without my having to match him every step of the way. The roads we were walking had very little traffic, but enough to endanger an unleashed dog. Brainstorm! I decided to drive Lance to the local park—the Delaware Water Gap

National Recreation Area—and let him loose in the woods. This forest had zero automobile traffic and Lance could run himself ragged without forcing me to run myself ragged right alongside him. Another plus in my view: he would get to be truly free for the first time in his life.

In hindsight, there was something reckless about doing this. For one thing, I didn't advise his owners of my intentions. For another, this dog had been tethered every day of his life since he was only a few weeks old; I had no idea what he would do if let loose.

On the day in question, I leashed Lance, took him off his run, and walked out onto the road. However, this time I led him to my car parked in front of our apartment and opened one of its doors. Lance jumped right in and immediately made himself at home on the front passenger seat, as if he'd ridden in cars a million times before. All seemed copacetic.

I turned on the engine and proceeded to inch out onto the road. From the second my car started moving, a barking and jumping marathon began. Lance leapt from the front seat to the back seat to the front seat to the back seat—well, you get the picture. He barked at pedestrians we passed. He barked at moving cars. He barked at parked cars. He just barked and barked, only occasionally stopping to catch his breath. My poor eardrums! It seems dogs can bark endlessly without getting hoarse. Too bad.

Every so often, he'd leap onto my lap attempting to get at someone or something he had spotted. This hampered my ability to drive as I had a seventy-pound whirlwind blocking my view and thrashing about wildly. Sometimes his paws activated the headlights, windshield wipers or emergency signals.

At one point, with Lance on my lap and his front paws haphazardly draped over the steering wheel, I happened to spot a pedestrian stopped in his tracks, scratching his head and staring at us, his face wrinkled in disbelief, no doubt wondering if some wacko (that would be me) was trying to teach a dog how to drive.

Dog, man and car forged on.

Once we reached the parking lot at the recreation area near the foot of Mount Minsi, I leashed Lance while still inside the car to make sure that, upon exiting, he wouldn't immediately disappear into the deep forest never to be seen again. I let him out of the car and off we went.

After walking a good distance on a marked trail, we turned off the beaten path and headed into the woods. I briefly debated with myself before unleashing Lance. *What if he runs off? What if he gets lost? He's not my dog. How would I be able to explain anything to the Schmidts? How would they react?* When the debate in my head ended, I concluded that letting him run was what I had brought him to the park for. My sense of adventure got the best of me. I set him free. He roamed a bit but, to my great relief, didn't head off into parts unknown. Rather, he went about his business while keeping me within his tracking range. We walked deeper into the woods, with Lance never wandering out of my sight.

Following a solid one-hour trek, we headed back towards the parking lot. Upon reaching my car, a Mexican standoff began. Still unleashed, Lance backpedaled as soon as I opened the car door and encouraged him to get in. Then, when I walked away from the car, he cautiously followed me, keeping enough distance to avoid being leashed. When I again headed back toward the car, he tagged along to a point, but came to halt when he realized what I was up to. This game went on for some time and, with no end in sight, I went to Plan B. After getting into my car and starting it up, I headed slowly down the dirt road leading to the park exit. Lance began following me. My hope was that at some point I'd stop and be able to coax him into entering my vehicle. However, each and every time the car braked and idled, Lance braked and idled. This strategy, too, was a failure. I sensed he was ready to bolt at any moment. Here I was, standing in a thickly wooded national park, having let someone else's dog loose with little hope of corralling him. What the hell had I been thinking?

Panic set in. Try as I did, I couldn't come up with an alibi to give his owners. I could lie and say I hadn't taken him that morning, but what if they'd seen me? One thing about the Schmidts: they kept an extremely low profile. Their house had a deserted look even when they were home. Prior to meeting Mr. Schmidt, I hadn't seen one human being on their property in the three-plus years I'd lived in Mount Bethel. There was no way to be sure that none of the Schmidts had seen me leaving with Lance earlier in the day. I could say we were walking in the neighborhood when he saw a deer and broke the leash to give chase. Would that fly? Maybe, maybe not. Then there was Anna. No matter what excuse I came up with, she'd be heartbroken. The truth was I had violated her trust.

Plan C. I parked, exited the car, and began walking toward a nearby wooded area. *Would Lance believe we were off on another hike?* Sure enough, he followed me. Once well into the woods, I sat myself on a rock and, when he came over to me, seized the chance to leash him. Success! We walked, somewhat dutifully on Lance's part, back to my car. His reluctance to be re-leashed and brought back home was obvious. Perhaps freedom tasted especially sweet to a dog like Lance.

On the way home, I endured *Barking and Jumping Marathon—the Sequel*. Lance kept his nose pressed to the window and eyes on the lookout for prey, barking at everything that moved and many things that didn't, like fire hydrants, mailboxes and telephone poles.

For the very first time in his life, Lance had been allowed to run free. Keeping that in mind, he behaved better than one would have had a right to expect. The bottom line is that I had let Lance loose and, although requiring some trickery on my part, he came back to me.

After this episode, I decided to forego walks on the road whenever possible, avoiding those tugs-of-war on the leash, and instead let Lance run loose in the woods around my neighborhood (or, on the trails surrounding Mount Minsi, if I was up for an eventful car drive). In either case, after wandering off to do "dog research," he'd always gravitate back to me. He soon lost his reluctance to be re-leashed. Maybe, just maybe, this dog was beginning to trust me.

One day, on our way back to the Schmidt property following a walk, a lady drove up to us, opened her window and, after looking at Lance and shaking her head as if in pity, turned to me and asked, "Did Anna tell you the whole story about this poor dog?"

"Yes, I guess so."

"It's disgusting, isn't it? Those people are criminals."

"I'm not sure—"

"I just want to tell you I think it's a wonderful thing you're doing for him. Just be careful. The Schmidts are…well, they're a disgrace in my book."

Hmm…this lady might have some useful information about Lance's past. Unfortunately, that thought didn't occur to me until she had driven away. I never saw her again.

Before long, Lance got into the habit of howling every time a walk ended and I headed home, pleading with me to come back and spend more time with him. Sometimes his tactic worked, compelling me to do an about-face and sit with him a while longer. After a few minutes, Lance would get bored with the inactivity. He'd strain on his run, getting as close as he could to the road. This was accompanied with healthy barking directed at me. Translation: *You've rested enough. Let's go!* My response? "Don't you ever get tired?" Lance always ignored that question. Sometimes, against my better judgment, I obliged with walk number two. Other times, I'd just continue to hang out and chat with him. Lance being a dog of few words, our conversations didn't last too long.

Whenever going home for good, I'd have to endure that pitiful wail the entire walk back to my apartment, some two blocks away. If Lance was trying to make me feel guilty, he was doing a great job of it.

During all my months of hiking with Lance, I never saw any of the Schmidts following that initial meeting with Jack. Not one of them ever phoned me to ask where I was taking Lance, how he was behaving, or if I ever let him loose. For my part, I volunteered none of that information.

-4-

Just Walkin' the Dog

As the winter of 2002 progressed, so did our hiking schedule. One trek led to another and before long, I was walking Lance three to four times a week. It was my way of trying to give this dog at least some measure of the exercise he so relished. Lance had obviously marked our hiking dates on his mental calendar, because now almost every time I approached the Schmidt property, he had already sensed my impending arrival and was straining at the end of his run, ready to go. Lance was dogmatic (sorry, I had to) about walking. I congratulated myself each time I accepted the challenge of exercising him and survived.

Despite my best efforts, every so often I couldn't hold up my end of the bargain. On those occasions, I pictured Lance waiting expectantly, in vain. Remorse set in. It got to the point that, because of my guilt, Lance would get walked on one of our days off, in order to make up for a scheduled day I no-showed. As for Lance, he never canceled.

Sometimes it took a huge effort to force myself away from the TV and recliner, reluctantly put on my sneakers, and drag myself up the road to the Schmidts, bracing myself for another grueling sojourn. Those who believe in karma might think I was getting my just reward for having jogged past Lance for all those years without inviting him to join me. Had Lance kept a count of all the walks we didn't take during that period? Was he intent on taking them all now that we had met? I wonder.

One day stands out. Heading up the hill to Lance's place, I spotted him already pulling on the lead, peeking at me around some bushes. His expression sent a clear message and he had a lot to say. *Boy, am I glad to see you! Finally! I was getting worried. Aren't you a bit late? Well, at least you stop*

26

now. Not like before when you'd run right by me and just keep going. I wonder what took you so long to catch on. Well, that doesn't matter now. Better to enjoy the present!

Walking a high-energy dog like Lance was definitely a lot of work. Was it becoming a labor of love?

-5-

First Things First

Weeks of walking Lance turned into months.

Every once in a while I'd think out loud in front of Clara, expressing my concerns about the dog's situation. I'd say things like: "You know, I feel good Lance is finally getting the exercise he needs. It's just that when I hook him back up, reality sets in." or: "I don't know if I'd even want the responsibility of owning a dog right now, but I'd feel a whole lot better if I was letting him inside someone's home when we were done hiking. Someone's, anyone's—even ours."

Why would the Schmidts have a neighbor feed and walk their dog all these years, unless they were all disabled? Of course, according to Anna, *she* was the one that had asked them if she could take care of Lance. I still only had Anna's side of the story. The only Schmidt I'd ever met, or even seen, was Jack. Our one, short conversation had been inconsequential. He'd given me a hinky feeling, but that alone didn't prove he was some kind of ruthless monster. It all seemed pretty screwy. Anna and the Schmidts—the odd couple.

Something *was* starting to sink in. Whether or not Lance's official owners abused him, they certainly neglected him. Except for our hikes and Anna's visits to feed him, Lance was living in a horrible mixture of isolation and exposure to potential injury. This was just flat-out wrong. In a sick way, Anna's charitable work all these years had been keeping Lance in harm's way while letting the Schmidts off the hook. Now, wasn't I part of the same scenario? What had I gotten myself into? Those characters had added me as another servant on their plantation and, just like Anna, I had volunteered to be one. Lance had a doghouse, food, and, thanks to me, he was getting plenty of exercise. Yes, the Schmidts were pulling off quite a stunt. Anna and I were doing all the grunt work as their stooges. For some time now it had puzzled me how Anna was able to handle the bizarre relationship she and the Schmidts had, and now here I was participating in it. Was I really helping Lance enough? At all?

Although feeling like a gofer, the idea of no longer walking this dog was out of the question. We would take hikes until at least one of us no longer could. Because Clara and I didn't own him, and we were living in an only-cats-allowed apartment, his less than ideal living situation would have to remain unchanged. The Schmidts, Anna, and Lance. I'd just keep hanging out with the sanest of the group, Lance, and leave it at that for now.

One day, after having just walked Lance, I came home more troubled than usual. Clara patiently listened to my tale of woe, how particularly bad I felt that evening leaving him stuck on his run. We asked ourselves what we could do to improve his situation.

We both had suffered recent bankruptcies and were very short on cash, so purchasing a house was not a likely option. I did a quick search on the Internet for any rentals in the area that were dog friendly. There were extremely few and those few commanded a small fortune in rent, plus an extra security deposit for a pet. Until we got our finances in order we, and Lance, would have to live with the status quo.

Clara went to the kitchen and proceeded to fry a large piece of beef liver. She suggested I go back to Lance and give it to him as a special treat. Smart woman. She was helping me ease my guilt.

Off I went to the Schmidts, carrying a baggie filled with liver. This would be a short visit, not another grueling march. My duties had been fulfilled earlier.

Speak of the devil! There he was, jumping up and down at the end of his lead. My showing up for a second time in the same day must've been an extra special occasion for Lance. I took the liver out of the baggie and let him grab it with his teeth. To my surprise, instead of immediately eating his treat, he carried it down to his food bowl. *Wow! What table manners. He's going to eat the liver in his "dining area."*

No, Lance had other ideas. He dropped the liver into his bowl and ran back up the hill in anticipation of—what else? —another walk. Apparently I hadn't paid my dues in full with our earlier trek. Who ever heard of a dog not instantly devouring fresh cooked meat already clenched in his teeth? Well, for this canine, walking trumped chow. I was definitely dealing with a different kind of dog.

Of course, I couldn't let him down so off we went.

Upon returning from our jaunt and being hooked up to his run, Lance bounded down to his food dish, grabbed the liver, and happily paraded back up the hill with the treat dangling from his mouth. He sat down next to me and gobbled it up in a matter of seconds.

At this point in his life, Lance was more starved for exercise, and companionship, than food.

-6-

So You Think You Can Dance?

Lance continued to impress me. However much he may have suffered physically over the years, there were few signs of wear and tear. Despite the neglect and isolation, he showed no bitterness. He was a very spunky dog.

Following one of our walks, I returned Lance to the Schmidts' property and hooked him up to his run. I made myself comfortable on the Schmidts' lawn and pulled out a biscuit for Lance, sitting alongside me. Instead of letting him take it directly from me, I decided to lay it on the ground in front of him. I assumed he'd snatch it right up. He didn't. He stared at it. Then he went for the treat with his mouth, but at the last minute, pulled back. Next, he began rolling his head around every which way possible.

What in the world is this dog doing?

Lance was kind enough to answer my question. Eyes still riveted on his treat, he started a ritualistic dance that I would witness countless times thereafter. While continuing to bob his head up and down and from side to side, he mixed in some fancy footwork. He sunk down on all fours and sprung himself into the air to his left. After landing, he sunk down again, and then propelled himself to the right. He went back and forth, performing a few sideways leaps in each direction. Again he lunged at the biscuit as if ready to snatch it, but at the last minute, backed off. He wasn't done dancing. He assumed a crouching position by lowering his front legs until they were flush with the ground and resting his head on top of his paws. While he was down in the front, his rump went way up in the back. Then, he leapt up on his hind legs, front paws waving in the air as if he were shadow boxing. He did this for a bit before sinking back down into the starting position. Then, up he went again. He repeated this balancing and paw-waving act several times. Throughout the entire performance, his head kept moving as if it were on a bobble toy, his eyes remaining fixed on his prize. When the floor show was finally over, Lance eagerly devoured the biscuit.

Had I just hallucinated? No. So how to explain what I'd just seen? Where did this act come from? How on earth could an untrained dog put together such a complex dance routine? The entire program appeared too polished and rehearsed to be spontaneous, but I was pretty sure Lance had never had a single dancing lesson in his life. It wouldn't surprise me if this was the first time in his life Lance ever performed these moves, finally feeling he had something to dance about. Either he'd kept this artistry on reserve, waiting for just the right moment to premiere it, or I was in the presence of an old dog that could teach himself new tricks. Whichever the case, with talent like that, if he was my dog, he would have been a television star by now. Lance's footwork deserved a name so I gave it one: the Aztec Side-step, a variation on the name of a seventies/eighties folk rock group (that would be the Aztec Two-Step, for you younger readers).

A few days later, we returned from another trek. Just for the heck of it, I started a little break dance of my own, very un-choreographed and extremely unprofessional. My hunch was correct. Lance—no treat required—immediately got into the spirit of things, showing off his more sophisticated gyrations. Ten-plus years old, and hard years at that, and here he was acting like a puppy. This dog was something else!

Eventually, it didn't matter where we were. If the mood struck me, I'd begin my amateurish jig, knowing Lance would join in. It did my heart good to watch him. He looked so happy that I'd briefly forget about what his first ten years must have been like. No doubt forgetting the past wasn't so easy for Lance. It probably was impossible.

Over the ensuing months, we continued to perfect our individual dancing styles, often on the Schmidts' lawn following a walk. I'm sure the neighbors were quite entertained by our stellar performances. As for the Schmidts, who knows what they thought of our antics? Who cares?

-7-

Homewrecker

During one of our now rare excursions solely on neighborhood streets (this particular day the woods were just too soaked following a torrential rainstorm), Lance and I passed by my apartment. On the spur of the moment, I decided to let him enter it. Why? I wanted to give Lance a treat. Assuming those first few weeks of his life in the Schmidt house had been no picnic, I thought I'd do a good deed. *We'll go inside my apartment and he can get a chance to relax for a while in the safety of a home for the first time in his life.* It seemed like a good idea. Good idea notwithstanding, it was probably better that Clara was not at home, as I was not so sure she would have been up for this kind of venture.

We had a split-level apartment featuring a bedroom, kitchen, and bath on the first floor, and a living room and additional bedroom on the second floor. The apartment had both a front and rear entrance.

After unleashing Lance, I opened the front door which led directly into the kitchen. From the moment he entered the apartment, it was as if a switch had been flipped in Lance's brain. All hell broke loose! He burst into a feverish foray throughout the apartment. Storming from room to room, he occasionally slammed on his brakes to sniff this or that, but nothing held his attention for more than a second or two. Then, it was off to the races again!

On one of his visits to the bathroom, Lance did make a pit stop for some quick liquid refreshment from the toilet. Thank God it had been flushed!

He wound up in the living room where he spotted Ashley, our cat, who was hiding behind my recliner. Lance went into overdrive and a dog-chasing-cat race ensued. In his pursuit of Ashley, Lance knocked over a TV table, a lamp table complete with lamp, and a vase filled with flowers and water.

Mesmerized by the chaos, all I could do was stand in one place and watch. Finally, with Lance in such a frenzy and fearing that our cat was about to become minced meat, I stopped gaping and rushed to open the back door. Under normal circumstances, Ashley tended to dawdle when I opened the door to let him in or out, but there was nothing normal about today's circumstances. No sooner had the back door been opened then Ashley was gone with the wind. Slamming the door behind me, I turned my attention to corralling Lance. With no cat to chase, he resumed scooting from room to room. During one of those scoots, I grabbed him by the collar and leashed him. Out the door we went. End of experiment.

The moment we were outside the flipped switch un-flipped; Lance regained his sanity. I returned him to his run and hurried back to the apartment. I had some cleaning up to do before Clara got home.

Anna was absolutely right. This dog couldn't last five minutes in a house. He was an outdoors dog for life.

-8-

Lance Makes a Big Splash!

A BORDER COLLIE IS UP FOR ANYTHING.

— FROM AN INTERNET SITE

A mid-May morning around 7:00 a.m. An unseasonably cool (low 40s) and blustery day. I took Lance for a stroll in a nearby woods we had visited a few times before. Today, I felt adventurous and decided to take an alternate path, one we had never before set foot on. A half hour later, we reached the trail's end and walked out into a clearing dominated by a huge pond. This was all new territory for Lance and, anxious to start his research, he hopped around excitedly, making it a job unleashing him. Once set free, he eagerly undertook an exploratory journey along the shoreline.

Ever on the alert, Lance spotted a swan resting on the water's surface. He began barking at it, all the while feverishly pacing back and forth along the water's edge. He appeared to be weighing the pros and cons of entering the water in order to give chase. Up and down the shoreline he scooted, continuing to assess the situation. Every once in a while, he lunged toward the water as if about to enter; then, he'd back off. I could hear his wheels turning: *Do I or don't I take the leap?* Big bodies of water were totally new to Lance. Would he dare enter this one?

At last, his mind made up, Lance jumped in with gusto and, like an Olympic champion, began swimming towards the swan. While furiously dog-paddling, he maintained a continual full-throated barking directed at his just-out-of-reach prey. Every time he neared his target, the swan did not fly away; he simply propelled himself forward just enough to remain out of Lance's reach as if he was taunting his pursuer. This game of cat and mouse or, rather, dog and swan, continued for a while until both hunter and hunted were far off shore.

Tiring of the exercise, the swan flew away, leaving Lance alone in the middle of the pond. I called to "my" dog, urging him to swim back towards the shore where I was standing.

Lance had other plans. He spotted a huge boulder jutting out of the water. As I watched from on shore, he swam over to it and, dripping wet, awkwardly scaled the mammoth rock to its tip. I ran along the shoreline up to the point where it was closest to this boulder, which sat some thirty yards away. After praising Lance for his rock-climbing skills, I encouraged him to come down, figuring he could then reenter the water and head for shore. Although he had managed to climb to the top of the extremely slippery boulder, he was clearly hesitant to try coming back down it. Instead, Lance stood on its peak, desperately trying to keep his balance while wailing mournfully at this dilemma of his own making. Imagine: the big, brave hunter frozen with indecision.

After months of letting Lance loose in the woods without incident, my luck had just run out. If I didn't get him off that rock, I'd have to report my recklessness to the Schmidts. The last thing I wanted to do was plunge into a bone-chilling pond, but, since Lance wasn't budging, I had no choice. After reluctantly taking off my sneakers and socks, I rolled up my sweatpants and waded out to the rock where Lance was pathetically perched. I was in knee-deep water while Lance, still howling, stood twenty feet above me, wobbling precariously atop the "mountain" he had so brashly climbed. No matter how I begged and pleaded, all my words of encouragement fell on deaf ears; Lance wouldn't move. Seeing no other option, I began to crawl up the slick rock on all fours. The plan upon reaching him? I hadn't the foggiest.

As I slowly climbed upward on all fours, Lance, finally getting his courage up, began to take some tentative steps, nervously edging downward toward me. He quickly lost his footing and went into a slide he couldn't stop. I lifted my hands up, preparing to corral him on his way down. No such luck. He barreled into me, and the collision caused us both to skid down the remainder of the exposed rock and fall into the water. Now I was as drenched as Lance was. What camaraderie!

The moment I rose up out of the pond, my water-logged clothes were greeted by a biting wind, chilling my bones to the core. Soaked man and animal waded side by side to shore.

This dog had a bit of daredevil in him. I liked that. We were a good match.

Nothing like a brisk walk home in windy, chilly weather while soaking wet. Judging from his wagging tail and happy strut, I had the strongest suspicion Lance did not share in my discomfort.

Just as we came to the Schmidt property Clara happened to drive by.

"Your pants are soaked. In fact, you're totally drenched."

"Don't even ask."

Clara looked at me disapprovingly. "Did you let him loose?"

"Just for a swim."

"How often do you let him run loose?"

I lied. "This was the first time. I figured I'd give it a shot."

"And you both got drenched. Not smart. You keep forgetting…he's not your dog."

"(Defensively) I know. I know."

After describing our escapade in more detail to her, Clara had to laugh. She decided the adventurers deserved a photograph and snapped one.

The first swim of Lance's life had been a memorable one.

LANCE AND AUTHOR AFTER SWAN LAKE DIP

-9-
Help Me!

Just a few days after our Swan Lake adventure, I came out to my car and found you-know-who lying by the driver's door. It was clear that Lance had made a mental note of where I lived following his stormy visit to my apartment weeks earlier, but how on earth did he get loose?

Since it was a workday, there was no time to investigate. I ran back inside, returned to Lance with a leash, and walked him back to his run. The run and lead were intact and Lance had arrived at my place wearing his collar, so I still had no idea how he broke free. While hooking him back up, I asked Lance how in the world he had sprung himself. He played dumb.

As I hurried back towards my apartment, Lance's customary *How could you leave me?* wail was playing as background music. No time for sympathy. I asked myself why anyone would let him loose, especially in broad daylight. That seemed unlikely. He couldn't possibly detach the lead from his collar, could he? Time to read up on Border Collies.

In spite of approaching land speed records, I was late for work that day, thanks to Lance. I got a brief scolding from Donna, my supervisor, also thanks to Lance. After explaining to her what had happened, she laughingly said, "I gotta give you credit, Walt. That's one of the most creative excuses I've ever heard." Then, Donna asked me a few questions about Lance. Initially, I thought she was quizzing me to satisfy herself that my story wasn't a fabrication. When she started to talk about her own two dogs, I became sure of three things: she believed my story, she was a dog lover herself, and I was in the clear.

The following day, I called Anna and told her what had happened. "Oh," she said, "he's coming to your place now. He used to come to mine when he got loose." There was a bit of reluctant acceptance in Anna's voice; I had become Lance's favored caretaker. She said that in the past, he'd occasionally show up at her door dragging all or part of his run behind him. This time he had arrived at my place carrying nothing but his collar.

Anna too could not understand how he'd gotten free unless someone had let him loose on purpose, which she thought highly improbable. If no one set him free, then Lance was one heck of an escape artist. This was a mystery that would forever remain unsolved.

Less than a week later, Clara and I pulled up to our apartment following a Sunday drive and spotted a black and white dog next to the porch railing. For a moment I thought that one of the other tenants, disregarding the landlord's prohibition of dogs, had obtained one, and it just happened to be a Border Collie. As I approached him, the dog began to perk up and make the same happy gestures that Lance always did upon seeing me. It was Lance.

Cheryl, an apartment tenant, came outside and told us that, when she had come home earlier, Lance was already in the parking area, dragging a lead behind him. He barked at her while she sat in her vehicle working up the nerve to exit. When she finally got out of the car and proceeded toward her apartment, he followed her, circling Cheryl "as if he was trying to herd me."

Cheryl secured him with the rope and, not knowing to whom the dog belonged, called the local dog pound. She was advised that someone would come to collect the dog. I asked her to telephone the pound and advise them the dog was not a stray. Lance had come this close to being carted off and taken to the local ASPCA, which at that time was a kill shelter (talk about an oxymoron!).

Lance had his lead, some twenty feet long, attached to his collar. The unattached end was frayed. I used the lead as a leash and walked him back home.

When we got to his run, I secured him to what little of his lead was still attached to the run. The spot where the lead had been severed dangled at least eight feet above the ground. To chew the lead in half, Lance would have had to jump in the air countless times, each time taking another bite at the wire. If he hadn't done that, then this dog had pulled on a super strong, plastic-coated steel wire and snapped it in two with brute force. If that was the case, did he do it with or without a running start? How many attempts did he have to make? How did he accomplish it without hurting himself? Incredible and baffling. Another unsolved mystery.

I called Anna, letting her know what had happened. She told me her husband had just put up that brand-new run and lead three days earlier. We were both amazed by Lance's strength—and determination.

A few days later, during a walk, I had a heart-to-heart with Lance, lamely explaining to him the realities of living a dog's life—the Schmidts were his owners and, besides, my landlord didn't allow dogs. He appeared less than disinterested in my excuse-making.

Lance's escapes from the Schmidt property and subsequent arrivals at my place were designed to send me a message: *Hey Dummy! Don't you get it? Do I have to draw you a diagram? I'm trying to adopt you.* I was a bit slow on the uptake, to some extent purposefully. I didn't want to be bothered any more than I already was by this dog's situation. Besides, there was nothing anyone could do to change it, at least not that I was aware of.

-10-

Dodging Bullets

Another day, another venture into the unknown. Actually this particular excursion found us in the partially known. Lance and I were walking on a path that took us past "Swan Lake," my name for the body of water in which Lance had initiated the first swim of his life. Much better weather today: a warm, clear, and dry spring day, five p.m.-ish. If he decided to go for a dip, at least this time the water wouldn't be so cold if I had to rescue him again.

Once unleashed, instead of heading for the water he wandered off into the woods to explore, while I stayed on the well-traveled path that headed who knows where. As I continued along by myself, the only sounds were an occasional wind-generated rustle of newborn leaves mixed with the chirping of birds.

This tranquility was broken by the unmistakable sound of Lance's barking off in the distance. He didn't respond to my calls; it was apparent that whatever had caught his attention was keeping it. I hustled back to the spot where we had parted ways. All the while Lance was still barking, even more excitedly than before.

Reaching the spot where I had unleashed him, I attempted to enter the woods through the same mass of bramble bushes Lance had disappeared into earlier.

I hadn't made much progress when, hearing heavy panting, I turned my head around and found Lance standing behind me on the path. He was extremely animated, jumping this way and that. His message: *"Follow me and I'll show you what I found!"* Sensing that was not a wise option, I hooked him up and began to jog briskly along the path heading towards a paved road.

Once back into civilization, I slowed the pace to a walk, anticipating an uneventful trip back to his place.

We had come to within fifty or so yards of our destination, when a speeding pickup truck pulled alongside us and came to a screeching stop. The driver, who looked like he was straight out of the movie *Deliverance* (right down to his missing teeth), rolled down the passenger window and threatened, "If I ever see that f------ dog again, I'll shoot him and then I'll come lookin' for you." My guess is he wasn't kidding. I noted there was a rifle rack, complete with two rifles, inside his truck's cab.

Before I could say a word, he drove off. The thought occurred to me that this angry stranger might have second thoughts and decide to come back and do me in right then and there. It was time to get off the streets. After leaving Lance, no doubt oblivious to the trouble he had stirred up, on the Schmidt property, I walked home, a bit more briskly than usual and happy to still be alive.

What had Lance stumbled upon? He'd wandered into a vast wooded area that had only a few dirt trails and no paved roads. We lived in a rustic area, the kind favored by methamphetamine producers. There had been several recent drug raids in nearby towns like Wind Gap and Pen Argyl. Perhaps he had come across a meth lab or maybe a bootlegger's operation. Whatever the case, that particular neck of the woods was immediately eliminated from our itinerary.

This dog was a lightning rod for the unexpected.

-11-

Death Defying

Dutifully, I headed up the road from my place to the Schmidt property. A bit behind (Lance's?) schedule, it was early evening and the sun was well into setting. No flashlight—this was going to be a short jaunt, if I had my way. Just another walk among a seemingly endless and growing string of walks.

By now, we had such a consistent routine that I expected Lance to be waiting impatiently for me on the edge of the Schmidt property, excitedly tugging at the end of his run. However, when I arrived this time, he was nowhere to be seen. In the growing darkness I couldn't see if he was in his doghouse, which sat well back off the road, but I assumed he was. I made the clucking sound with my tongue that usually sufficed to alert him to my presence. There were still no signs of life. This was not like Lance.

After I called his name several times, he finally appeared from his doghouse and began slowly walking, not running, up the sloping lawn towards me.

Once Lance got closer, I saw the problem. He had a gash that went from his forehead through his upper and lower eyelid, continuing on along his snout. There were numerous patches of caked blood on his face. The perpetrator, whoever or whatever, had come dangerously close to destroying Lance's eye.

Even in such pitiful condition, he was as eager as ever to go on a hike. Instead, I took him the few short blocks to Anna's home. She took one look at Lance and said, "I'll take care of this." Leaving him with her, I headed back home. On the way, two questions haunted me: what, or who, had done this to Lance, and how many times had something like this happened to him in the past?

The next day I called Anna to get Lance's medical update. The previous night she had insisted that Mr. Schmidt drive the dog to the veterinarian and, after a heated argument, he did. Lance had been treated and hopefully there would be no permanent eye damage.

After allowing Lance several days to recuperate, I went to walk him, bracing myself for what I'd find. It was late in the day and the sun was going to sleep. Nearing my destination, I began picking up on a conversation that was taking place on the Schmidt property. I slowed my pace and lingered at the yard's edge, keeping out of sight behind some foliage. I could barely make out Mr. Schmidt and, presumably, one of his sons hovering over their dog. As they applied what I assumed was medication for his injuries, Lance yelped in discomfort. Each time he did, the two men seemed to take delight, or maybe that was just my imagination.

"That's it for me. From now on that bitch can come over here and baby this mutt. He's not my problem. I got better things to do. Hey, remember that Fourth when you and Al wrapped him up in all those one-and-a-halfers [fireworks]? I never knew a dog could jump like that. Then he was rolling around on the ground like an asshole trying to get them off. What a stupid mutt. This effin' dog costs me more than he's worth. I should do myself a favor and put him out of his goddamn misery for good."

"F--- yeah," his son agreed. "That jerk-off that walks him all the time would be heartbroken. (Faking sympathy) Boo hoo."

"Hey, if we get rid of the doghouse and run, he'd come to the door and I'd say, 'What dog? I don't own any dog. What the hell ya talkin' about? Whadda ya nuts? Do I know you?'"

They both chuckled.

I stood nervously poised to interrupt their laugh-fest, but, just as I began to step out from behind the bushes, they started walking away.

Not being the confrontational type, I waited in the shadows while the two men laughed themselves silly all the way back into their house.

I called to Lance and he ran up the lawn to meet me. Other than the open slits on his upper and lower eyelid, he didn't look too bad compared to the bloody mess he was just days earlier. Lord only knows what this dog had fought with. He insisted that we take a walk, so we did.

On the way back to my apartment I gave myself a few good swift kicks. How could I have been so dense? I finally—and belatedly—realized, once and for all, just what a precarious position Lance was in. Against her best wishes and despite her hard work, all those years Anna had unwittingly kept throwing Lance a life preserver that kept him afloat in a pool of sharks. Every time we finished a walk, I too was leaving him in harm's way. Left alone to defend himself, his mobility and maneuverability were severely limited by his run. Furthermore, a doghouse with a wide open front was no place to seek safety from an enemy attack. Besides, if he was taking on a bear, for example, it was a mismatch from the get-go.

Then there were the Schmidts. Witnessing them in action that night, I didn't like what I saw or heard. This evening's scenario struck me as exceptionally perverse. They had been administering medical treatment to a dog while joking about killing him. I had thought of them as neglectful oddballs. I shouldn't have. Obviously, they were capable of anything. It was time to stop respecting the Schmidts' ownership rights so much.

Whatever my feelings were about Lance's situation prior to this day, they now included a sense of urgency. It was crystal clear. Sooner or later his number would be up.

Later that night Clara and I talked about Lance's plight. At some point I blurted out, "That dog is not going to die under *my* watch!" I had made up my mind. We were going to become Lance's new owners, by hook or crook. If for some reason the Schmidts would not voluntarily relinquish him, I decided I would take Lance unannounced. Before that evening, the idea of stealing someone's dog had never once in my life occurred to me. Not sure how to even go about such thievery and hoping I wouldn't have to, I found myself including it among my options. At this point, Lance's life might depend on my committing larceny.

The following day I phoned Anna letting her know of our intention to take Lance in. She was overjoyed and assured me his owners would gladly relinquish their dog. I didn't disclose the urgency of the situation fearing Anna might overreact, confront the Schmidts, and inadvertently put Lance's life in even greater jeopardy.

We again began searching—this time in earnest—for a house to rent or, if at all possible, purchase, that was not in the Mount Bethel area. After all, it wouldn't make sense to continue living in the area with a dog stolen from a neighbor. That, of course, was a worst-case scenario. I, like Anna, had little doubt that the Schmidts could care less about their dog and would be happy to get him off their property.

Was it at all feasible for us to purchase a house? The results of a credit check turned out to be encouraging.

My sister Liz had been following our exploits with Lance. I got on the phone with her. "Liz, you know I'm not big on melodrama but I'm telling you…I used to just think that dog was in a bad spot, but he's really in a lethal spot. His owners are absolute sickos. They were joking about nuking him. I'm not even sure they were joking."

Three days later, her check arrived covering an estimated down payment and closing costs. Knowing what a dog lover she was, I am confident Liz was as intent on helping save Lance's life as she was on helping Clara and I become homeowners. That was perfectly understandable to us.

We began weekend searches for the right kind of home. Over several weeks, we viewed many houses, none of which fit our, or rather Lance's, needs.

Then, one Saturday, we drove to an address in Canadensis, Pennsylvania, suggested by a local realtor. As soon as I pulled our car into the driveway of 21 Oak Tree Drive, I turned to Clara and said "Sold!" before even looking inside. Why? Located on a low traffic cul-de-sac, the house was surrounded on three sides by undeveloped woods. It was also within walking distance of the Delaware State Forest. This was the perfect spot for Lance. We overlooked the fact that the house needed a huge amount of work, the kitchen was miniscule, and the yard was loaded with huge, dead trees sitting precariously close to the house and ready to fall at any second. We picked a place to live in based on a dog's preferences.

Contracts were signed and June twentieth was set as the tentative closing date. We scheduled a week later as move-in day for Lance. Somehow, in all the excitement, I forgot about his less-than-successful visits to Anna's house and our apartment.

The countdown began. Which would come first, Lance's rescue or his death? I began checking on him daily, just to confirm his continued existence. Of course, Lance wouldn't settle for a mere visit; a grueling walk had to be included, too. Each day while heading for the Schmidt property and fearing what I might find, I prayed to the patron saint of dogs, not knowing his name or if he even existed; I was just covering all bases. Finding Lance waiting near the curb brought relief, but not complete relief until a closer inspection revealed no new wounds. If he wasn't already in sight, I didn't relax until my clucking sound brought him barreling out of his doghouse and up the hill.

Lance had little idea what his owners might have in store for him. On second thought, considering how they had mishandled him over the years, maybe he did. Whether he was concerned or not, I did enough worrying for both of us.

To add to the suspense, just when we were getting ready to take him, the original closing date was postponed for a week.

There wasn't much else to do but mark days off the calendar. There was nothing of substance for me to report to any authorities that would make Lance's life any safer. To confront the Schmidts at this point would only make things worse. Since we were still living two blocks down the road, stealing Lance was pointless. His life, up for grabs as it had been for so long, was in the hands of fate, luck or God—take your pick.

Clara and I were nervous wrecks. My walks with Lance now had a surreal air to them. I was exercising a dog that I might find dead the next day. How in the world had Anna dealt with this kind of stress for all those years?

Lance was a dead dog walking. But, hadn't he always been?

-12-

Homeward Bound

Clara and I moved into our new home near the end of June. A couple of days later, I drove back down to Mount Bethel to exercise Lance. After our walk I explained to him that he'd be moving in with us over the upcoming weekend. Lance wagged his tail, as dogs will do, allowing me to believe he understood me.

Saturday, July sixth was a sweltering hot day. It was time to get Lance. I drove to the Schmidts' residence. Lance was lying alongside his doghouse. Recognizing my car, he perked up. Though relieved to see he was still very much alive, there was no time for celebrating. I had business to attend to.

Walking up the driveway, I entered an alternate universe, a domain controlled by those strange aliens who went by the name Schmidt. They didn't really know me and I didn't really know them. I had never once discussed Lance's situation with them. Suddenly, the whole idea of taking their dog struck me as bizarre, surreal, and ridiculous.

Then it hit me. My old nemesis, the panic attack. *I can't handle this. I'm going to collapse. Turn around. Go back to the car and regroup—or just go home.*

I never got to take the easy way out and reverse course. All the while my mind was screaming "Retreat!", my feet were braver and marched me forward. Just like that, butterflies and all, I found myself at the front door, introducing myself to a middle-aged woman with dark hair and olive skin whom I presumed to be Mrs. Schmidt. Throughout our brief conversation, she kept her right eyebrow arched in a way that created a look of bewilderment, disbelief, and distrust all rolled into one.

"Hello. My name's Walter. I'm the guy who has been walking your dog the past few months."

"Yes?"

"I recently purchased a house and I'd like to take your dog with me. It's got a large property; it's on a low traffic street and—"

"Oh, I couldn't let you do that. Lance is a part of our family. I'm going to have brain surgery soon, you know."

"I'm sorry to hear that. I hope all goes well."

End of conversation. I was left speechless, unable to think of anything clever enough to counter Mrs. Schmidt's delusion that she loved her dog. Whatever the origins of the other members of Mrs. Schmidt's family, our brief exchange combined with her facial expression convinced me she was from the farthest reaches of outer space.

Dumbfounded, I took my leave, returned to my car, and headed back to Canadensis, soaked in sweat from the heat and my anxiety. No need to visit Lance in the backyard. Why give him the bad news?

I felt like a fool. We had just traded an apartment that cost $450 a month (heat included) for a $750 mortgage (nothing included), all for the sake of a dog, a dog that wasn't even ours. Now, that dog wasn't moving in. My foolish feeling morphed into a troubled feeling. Would I keep walking Lance, necessitating a lengthy car ride each time I did? Or, would I just forget about him? *But wait! What the hell was I thinking about? Walking this dog wasn't the issue. The Schmidts might very well kill him!*

Ultimately, my combination of feelings boiled down to one—anger. How could this woman call "a part of the family" a dog her family hadn't fed, hadn't walked, and had not let into their house since he was a weeks-old puppy? If anything, he was a part of Anna's family. Nothing had prepared me for Mrs. Schmidt's off-the-wall response to my request. Granted, I had never advised her or any member of her family as to my plans. In fact, I hadn't spoken to any of the Schmidts after that initial meeting with Jack, but how on earth could they object to finally getting Lance off their property? Did they get so much enjoyment out of mistreating their dog that they'd miss having him around for the entertainment value? I felt extremely disheartened and growing angrier by the second. After getting home, I called Anna and let her know of Mrs. Schmidt's inexplicable inflexibility.

"What?! That's ridiculous! Let me handle this. I'll call you back in a little while."

I sat in my recliner and stewed. I tried to convince myself that Anna would be able to reason with the Schmidts. But what if she couldn't? My anger was now fostering criminal calculation—if necessary, I would steal Lance.

Not having stolen anything since my shoplifting days as an adolescent, I figured to be a bit rusty on technique. Caution was critical. If the dog immediately disappeared it would be rather obvious who had taken him. To be on the safe side, I might have to wait several months—*would Lance survive that long?*—before making my move. I'd stake out the Schmidt residence to see if there was any period of time during the day when all of its occupants were not at home. Or maybe I'd take Lance in the dead of night. Could he be trusted to keep his mouth shut during such an operation?

There was a further consideration regarding the Schmidts. They were definitely crazy people. What if they happened to be crazy people with firearms?

To complicate matters further, I wasn't sure Clara would be as enthused as I was about committing robbery.

Then, there were the legal ramifications. What if I got caught? I was the drug and alcohol counselor at the local correctional facility. A judge might decide that I should be living with, instead of treating, the inmates and possibly need therapy myself. I visualized the headlines in the local newspaper: "Jail Counselor Jailed."

A few hours passed before I got a call from Anna. I wouldn't have to break the law.

"You can take Lance."

Anna told me that she had warned Mrs. Schmidt that if she didn't let me take their dog, the following would happen: she would stop feeding him and then contact authorities, charging the Schmidts with animal neglect and abuse. My guess is Anna was bluffing, as I don't think it would have been possible for her to completely abandon Lance under any circumstances. If it *was* a bluff, thank God it worked.

I broke the speed limit driving back to Mount Bethel, fearful Lance's flaky owners might change their minds. I met Anna and a few other Mount Bethel neighbors at the Schmidt residence. Together, we loaded the run and the dog house—the thing weighed a ton!—onto a pickup truck. Thankfully, none of the Schmidts at home did more than occasionally peek from this or that window. I let Lance into my car and both vehicles proceeded to our new home. As always, he barked and jumped around endlessly during the entire trip.

Upon arrival in Canadensis, he burst out of my car and, tugging on his leash, began feverishly sniffing every bit of the new terrain he could get his nose on. As soon as the doghouse and the run were set up in the backyard, I hooked Lance up to his lead. After thanking them for their help, Anna and my old neighbors left. Clara and I then went into the house to relax a bit.

Before we could get comfortable, the howling began. I went to the side door that opened to the backyard and saw Lance straining on his run. The message was clear. He wanted to come into the house. Had he decided he'd lived outside long enough? Did he sense there was more security inside? Had he become that attached to me? Even if "Yes" was the answer to all these questions, we were concerned about taking in an older dog that had never been housebroken, hoping to delay that task for at least few days. Lance, however, would simply not stop barking, so we decided to bring him into the house in the name of peace and quiet.

I went outside and, after unhooking his lead, walked him up the side stoop. Up popped a mental picture of him scurrying around our Mount Bethel apartment. Opening the door, I warned Clara to brace herself for Lance's stampede throughout the house. It didn't happen. Upon entering, he initiated a spirited, thorough, and quick search of our home and then sat down in the living room, his back to the fireplace, in a state of vigilance. His positioning allowed him to view the front and side entrance doors, the living room, the kitchen, part of the laundry room, and the hallway leading to the two bedrooms. Possibly most critical for Lance, his location allowed him to easily watch both Clara and me. I thought to myself, *Hey! This isn't so bad. At least he's not the tsunami he was in the apartment.*

That first day I took Lance on three to four lengthy walks to protect against his urinating or defecating inside the house. Amazingly, in all the time Lance would live at 21 Oak Tree Drive, he relieved himself perhaps two times in the house. A dog that had spent the first ten years of his life outside housebroke himself.

-13-

Damaged Goods

Talk about a rude awakening!

Considering the chaotic nature of his first encounter with Lance, it was no surprise our cat Ashley had spent that first day in Canadensis keeping a low profile outside the house. Shortly before midnight, Clara got up to see if he was at the door. Walking through the unlit kitchen, she took care as she stepped over Lance. It didn't matter. He leapt up and bit her on the wrist. Clara let out a scream that jarred me awake. I rushed out to the kitchen, turned on the lights, and found her standing alone, blood dripping from her arm. After cleaning and dressing the wound, we gave each other a hug for moral support.

First, Clara expressed her doubts. "I'm not so sure about this dog."

Then she began to make alibis for him. "I must have startled him. I should've turned on the kitchen light first. I should've called his name."

Where was the dog? I walked into the living room and turned on a table lamp. There, on the other side of the room, sat Lance in the same defensive position he had taken earlier that day. Before I could complete three steps towards him, he let out a sinister growl that stopped me in my tracks. His upper lip curled, giving me a clear view of a canine's canines. I retreated back into the kitchen.

We decided that the only thing to do for the moment was to go back to bed. Fortunately, to do that we didn't have to pass close by Lance. We briskly scooted into the bedroom and I even more briskly closed the bedroom door behind us.

After getting into bed, and though totally exhausted, neither of us could fall asleep. We lay awake talking about the wild dog that was roaming the house. Clara was extremely upset. I did my best to act calm, hoping that would lessen her stress.

I got up and locked the bedroom door. Sleep then came quickly.

5:30 a.m. the next day. Neither of us was ready to wake up, but an incessant scratching at our door forced us to. *Oh, that's right. Last night we went to sleep with Cujo in the next room.* What to do? If I jumped out the bedroom window, about a fifteen-foot drop, I'd be able to go to the front door and coax Lance from the house. Then, I'd rush back inside, leaving Lance outside. At that point we could decide what to do next. Looking out the bedroom window, I saw there was a slew of cinderblocks on the lawn waiting to greet my arrival. A bit too risky for my taste.

Meantime, the scratching on the door continued. I told Clara to get on the bed for safety. I was going to check to see what kind of mood Lance was in.

Up on the bed went Clara. I cautiously opened the door. With it slightly ajar, I saw Lance standing in the hallway. As I stepped back and turned to say something to Clara, Lance helped open the door the rest of the way by jumping up and pushing on it with his front paws. The door was now wide open. He didn't attack me. Instead, he began moving backwards towards the side exit door, prancing along the way. I followed at a safe distance. *Last night he scares us out of our wits and now here he is doing that damn happy dance of his.*

Lance made it clear he wanted to go outside. I was glad to oblige so we both left the house and headed into the woods. I didn't bother to leash him. There was no way I was putting my hands anywhere near him.

Once outside, Lance was his old frisky self, maybe even a bit more since this was all new territory for him to explore. It was hard for me to believe the dog I was with was the same one that had terrorized us the night before.

When we got back home, I yelled to Clara, "He seems okay. Get ready!" I let Lance back in and he went to the living room taking his now customary sitting-up-against-the-wall-with-eyes-peeled-on-us position.

We spent the rest of the morning walking on eggshells. We were trapped inside a cage with a wild animal.

Later that afternoon, I was sitting in my recliner watching television. Lance left his position of watchfulness and sat down beside the arm of my chair. With my eyes still on the TV screen, I absentmindedly patted him on his head. He whipped around, growled, and tried to bite me. It was an unsuccessful attempt only because, just in time, I reflexively jerked my hand out of his rapidly closing jaw. Even so, my hand was left sporting a detailed impression of his teeth, complete with foaming saliva. Meanwhile, he rushed away to reassume a defensive stance in front of the fireplace.

Sensing Clara had not seen all this, I didn't tell her about it. If I had, Lance would've been on even thinner ice than he already was.

What kind of dog asks to be petted and then snaps at the person offering affection? Was I a friend or foe in Lance's eyes? Or, was I both?

Anna had told me that Lance had bitten her only one time when she had inadvertently touched a "sore spot." He had never shown any signs of viciousness towards me when he was living outside at the Schmidts' place. Sure, there was the one time he'd turned and briefly growled at me when I patted him while he was eating, but that had seemed understandable, an animal protecting his food supply, something he'd probably been forced to do for many years. Could Lance have sized me up as his potential savior, put himself on his best behavior until rescued and, once safely inside our home, let his evil twin brother out of the closet? That seemed a bit of a stretch, even for the most calculating of dogs.

So many questions: how had Dr. Jekyll been able to suppress Mr. Hyde for seven months in Mount Bethel? Were all Border Collies that clever or just Lance? Why would he start biting now? Where was his gratitude? I feared Lance was turning out to be too big an undertaking.

The next morning, I was preparing to leave for work. Clara had left earlier for her job. Lance, resting comfortably on our bed, looked the picture of contentment. I said "So long" and gently patted the back of his head. He whirled around and went for my hand with a vicious, toothy snarl. Quickly yanking my hand out of harm's way, I froze in place, not knowing what he would do next. I was in a room with a wild beast. Pulling myself together, I left the house wondering exactly what had I gotten Clara and myself into.

I drove to work a nervous wreck, thinking about our lunatic dog. Only hours after having pleaded to be let into our house, he bit Clara and subsequently went after me twice. Why had Lance never shown any tendency to bite while in Mount Bethel? Again, I asked myself if he could have been smart enough to hide his true nature until rescued. Was that possible?

In hindsight, Anna had told me Lance proved to be totally unfit to ever stay in her house. Somewhere along the way, I had also forgotten that his lone visit to my apartment in Mount Bethel turned out to be a complete fiasco. Perhaps I'd been blindly optimistic in my assessment of this dog.

Following Lance's rescue, several of the Schmidts phoned Anna, half-begging, half-threatening her, trying to get our address. Mrs. Schmidt, as delusional as ever, said she would need Lance as a therapy dog following her surgery. Anna pretended not to know our whereabouts. Clara and I agreed that, for the time being, Lance was ours for better or worse. Even though it looked like it was for worse, bringing him back to the Schmidts was not, nor ever would be, an option. We had bought (into) a damaged dog based on false advertising, but there was no humane return policy.

Having decided for the time being to carry on with Project Lance, I dismantled the run. The doghouse was never again used and instead offered to a local pet rescue organization. When they failed to respond, it was broken up for firewood.

The doghouse came down; the "Beware of Dog" sign went up. I was the proud owner of my first antisocial dog.

-14-
What is He?

Lance had taken us completely by surprise. What kind of dog did we have on our hands or, for that matter, had his *teeth* on our hands? Lance had made it clear he wanted no part of being stuck on a run. He also wasn't suited to live under a roof with humans. We now feared the dog we had grown to love.

Clara reasoned that, having done it for so long, Lance was more comfortable living outside, dangers and all. Rather than recognizing its potential for safety, living inside probably seemed strange and even stressful to him. That begs the question: Why did he insist on coming inside from day one with us?

Clara also felt Lance did not really know her that well yet. Possibly so, but I had already walked him regularly for seven months and he was threatening me, too. One thing we both agreed on: Hypervigilance had probably long ago become second nature for this dog.

Was Lance neurotic or psychotic? A neurotic dog may exhibit chronic anxiety, hyperactivity, fear, obsessive behavior, and inappropriate responses to stimuli. That described Lance. A truly psychotic dog exhibits acute, unpredictable and apparently uncontrollable changes in mood, behavior or personality that can tend to be dangerous and destructive to both the dog and other non-threatening animals and humans. That also described Lance. Erratic canine behavior is more likely to be diagnosed as psychotic if a dog's history includes, among other things, a history of severe beatings and/or extreme psychological trauma, both of which we now suspected Lance had experienced.

Isn't biting unannounced and without good reason both an inappropriate response to stimuli (neurotic) and also unpredictable behavior (psychotic)? Lance's behavior was destructive to others (psychotic), but he also showed remorse after many of his outbursts, as if he had just done something he wished he hadn't (both neurotic and psychotic). He did, on occasion, freeze in place and "leave us" for another world (psychotic), but only rarely and only for brief moments. To further confuse the issue, Valium, the one psychotropic drug we ever administered to Lance, had no apparent effect on him.

A call to a local veterinarian yielded some interesting information. The vet described Lance's seemingly aggressive acts as fear bites. He explained that, if forced to live constantly on the alert, a dog can feel threatened very easily and react instinctively, even in the absence of any tangible threat, seeing danger where there is none. Since Lance had been outside defending himself all those years, maybe he had come to believe that the best defense was a good offense. The vet said a Border Collie is usually good-natured, but lack of socialization and outlets for physical energy can leave him anxious and unreliable. The fact that his original owners were abusive added an additional layer of stress. Thus, the paradox: Lance was a biter, but not necessarily vicious by nature. It was nice to know that apparently none of this was personal, but it did nothing to allay our ongoing fears of being attacked.

When I asked the vet why Lance had been so well-behaved until getting to Canadensis, with a laugh he answered, "I'm a veterinarian, not a psychologist." I would have laughed along with him if I wasn't stuck living with this canine puzzle.

A domesticated animal is one sufficiently tame to live with people; it is comfortable when in close association with humans. Domestic dogs are characterized by their trainability, playfulness, and ability to fit into households and social situations. The majority of contemporary dog owners consider their dog as part of the family, with pet dogs playing an active role in family life. Many of these dogs have set tasks and/or routines as if they were a family member. Lance had never been a member of any family and he wasn't off to a good start with us.

If not a domestic animal, was Lance feral? A feral animal is one which has escaped from a domestic status and is living more or less as a wild animal. As a puppy, Lance did not escape from a domestic situation; he was banished from it. Furthermore, because of Anna's attention, he had not lived a completely feral life.

Was he semi-feral? A semi-feral animal lives predominantly in a feral state, but has some contact and experience with humans. Of course, the nature and quality of this contact and experience is critical. This semi-feral condition might be due to:

1. An animal's having been born into a domesticated state and then reverting to (or being forced into, as Lance was) more primitive living conditions, or

2. It might result from an animal's growing up in essentially wild conditions, but having developed a comfort level with humans (or, as in Lance's case, one human—Anna) due to feeding, receiving medical care, or similar contacts.

The life Lance had lived was some twisted combination of (1) and (2).

Dogs first had utility to early human hunter-gatherers and, over the years, they have helped humankind by herding, pulling loads, protecting, assisting police and military, and, so importantly, being family companions. Their huge, beneficial impact on society earned canines the moniker "Man's Best Friend."

Unfortunately for Lance, he had lived much of his life as if he were a wild creature. His only positive interaction with humankind was provided by visits from a neighbor. Other than those occasions Lance was either completely alone, being harassed, or—it now seemed likely—fighting for his life. Would it be a stretch to suggest that a dog might not be any more immune to the negative effects of isolation, neglect, and abuse than a human being?

All things considered, Lance was certainly not a domesticated animal, yet not a completely feral one either.

Once living with us, Lance probably didn't change as much as Clara and I did. Rather, we adapted to his unpredictability, which led to an abnormal owners-dog relationship. One example: we resolved to never again walk in, or into, our house if it was unlit and a lurking Lance awaited to greet us. We left lights on night and day, just to ensure the house never became completely dark. In case electricity was lost, there were flashlights on hand in every room and in both cars, should we have to enter a darkened house with Lance lying in wait. Paying the electric bill in a timely fashion became a top priority.

The threat of getting bitten at any moment became an ongoing fact of life. There were times when Lance acted as if he didn't even know us, let alone like us. Would we ever be able to trust the dog we had rescued? We assumed it would take some time for Lance to calm down—hopefully not too much time.

My guess is that the anxiety we experienced gave us only a small taste of the fear our dog dealt with since the day he was born.

-15-

Leashing the Beast/Exit Strategy

Thanks to Lance, "home is where the dog is" now sounded less like a warm and fuzzy slogan and more like a warning.

Hooking Lance to a leash had never been an issue in Mount Bethel; now it was. The first few days in Canadensis, we were too petrified to even try leashing our dog. Instead, I'd let him outside and make a mad dash for the woods. Fortunately, he'd happily follow me, instead of wandering onto the road or some neighbor's property.

Shortly thereafter, we devised a rather ingenious method of leashing the devil dog. I'd call Lance, telling him he was going for a hike ("You want to go bye-bye?"). He'd come running enthusiastically. As I got set to hook him up, Clara would get Lance to turn his head away from me and toward her by offering him a treat balanced on the end of a long serving spoon. That momentary distraction and, of course, my lightning reflexes, allowed me to hook him up. With the click of the leash, all thoughts of food vanished. Lance would charge towards the door, often leaving his treat untouched or only partially eaten. Besides being a maniac in general, Lance was a maniac for exercise in particular.

There were times I'd fumble my first attempt to leash him. During my follow-up try Lance was the big winner— he'd have to be offered a second treat. No doubt, we were rewarding our dog's menacing behavior. Anything to avoid being bitten.

We used this procedure for several weeks before I decided to put Lance, and myself, to the test. I hooked him up unassisted, all the while talking about the walk he was about to go on, keeping him in an up mood. The fact is Lance never bit or even threatened either of us once when he was being leashed. A leash signified he was going for a walk, so what's not to like? Lance was too happy to attack. The diversionary tactics with food had never been necessary other than to assuage our own fears.

Besides the leashing issue, another challenge was getting over the fear of entering the house when Lance was inside it. Would he consider us intruders?

We'd moved Lance to Canadensis on a Saturday. The next Monday was a workday for both Clara and me. During the late afternoon, I got a phone call at my workplace from my wife. She was already home from work, sitting in her car in the driveway. It hadn't dawned on her until getting close to home that she'd have to enter the house and deal with Lance alone. She found the prospect very unappealing.

"I can't go in the house. I'm afraid of that dog."

"I don't blame you. Just wait until I get home and we'll figure something out. It'll be another half hour, forty-five minutes."

"I'll do some shopping and see you back here around five-thirty."

Around that time, I pulled into the driveway. Clara was already there, waiting in her car. I got out of mine, walked over to hers, and got in. Clara was a nervous wreck. She said that day had been the first time in her life she'd been more eager to go to work than come home from it. I gave her hand a gentle squeeze in a show of support. We sat together and alternated between fretting over what to do and laughing at the ridiculousness of it all. I still was having a hard time believing this was the same dog I'd hung out with all those months in Mount Bethel. Clara was having a hard time period.

We exited the car and walked up the stoop next to the side door. I peeked inside. There was Lance, on the other side, waiting for us. His face was lit up, his tail wagging and he was anxiously jumping around—the very picture of a dog happy to see his owners.

"I'm going to open the door and try to enter. He looks okay to me. You wait here until the coast is clear. I'll let him come outside and then I'll run with him into the woods. You enter the house before we get back."

Clara went down the steps and moved away onto the lawn, giving Lance a wide berth. Neither of us had any idea what to expect from him.

Remaining on the stoop, I opened the screen door and then the inside door. Lance danced around, waiting for me to enter the house, just like any self-respecting dog would. Taking a deep breath and a leap of faith, I went inside. Lance kept his upbeat demeanor, so I cautiously and oh-so-briefly petted him.

Clara summoned up her courage and also entered. Lance rushed over to her. She too gave him a quick pat, on his tail. (Chicken!) With all the social niceties completed, next on Lance's agenda—what else? A walk. Entering our home had become a non-issue, as long as it wasn't dark inside.

Exiting a Lance-occupied house without him was a whole other matter. When Lance was inside, seeing either one of us head for the door triggered his wanderlust. Since neither Clara nor I dared to physically restrain him, we developed exit strategies. If one of us was leaving, the other would distract Lance with talk or a treat. Once we got over our fear of leashing Lance, we had another option: whoever was staying home would take Lance on a leash out the side door into the yard, wait for the other to escape from the front door, and then bring Lance back in. If only one of us was at home and wanted to leave, that would necessitate throwing a treat to the farthest corner of the living room and then flying out the door. An alternative: I'd sometimes loiter by the side door pretending to be busy straightening out canned foods on the shelf there. Then, I'd make a quick break for it. If both Clara and I were leaving, a combination of distracting talk, flinging treats, and pointless can-arranging might be utilized.

A few months went by before we tired of our own stratagems. One day, the two of us headed for the door to leave, purposely ignoring our dog. We wanted to see if these exiting games were still necessary. Lance signaled their end by staying put, without having to be fooled or bribed. By that time, we had spent a small fortune in treats.

Lance had settled in. We thought that meant he had also settled down. We were wrong.

-16-

Trying to Tame the Tiger

While still in Mount Bethel, we had hired an animal obedience trainer, Jan Bittner, to help us work with Lance. Jan was a believer in the controversial alpha theory that links dog behavior to that of wolf packs. The general idea: a canine, mimicking behavior seen in wolves, will strive to become top dog among the humans in his life. Owners must demonstrate dominance over dogs in their care or else be controlled by them. There's something unappetizing about this theory, at least to me. I appreciate a cooperative dog, but I do not believe obedience can only be obtained by winning some battle of wills. It is just not who I am. Upon learning that I sometimes let Lance run loose in the woods, Jan chided me for what she called my "freedom for animals" philosophy. Around her, I kept my opinions to myself. I recognized that, theories aside, Jan had some expertise that I didn't.

In the yard behind our apartment Jan and Clara watched as Lance, to Jan's surprise, calmly allowed me to place a Gentle Leader™ (the head collar that can help control lunging, pulling, and jumping) over his snout. Then I began walking, keeping him close to my side. When it was time to make a turn, I gave him a command and—lo and behold!—he turned with me. I also was able to have him sit and stay in place as I walked away. Jan was impressed at Lance's trainability in view of his age and background. He soon learned some basic commands: pivot, stay, sit, turn left, turn right, and come. Of course, people more familiar with the Border Collie breed than I wouldn't have been surprised that Lance was such a quick learner. They know Border Collies typically understand and internalize a command no later than the fifth time it is given.

Jan continued to stop by on a regular basis during our first few months in Canadensis, training now a critical necessity if we hoped to "cure" Lance.

She would hook Lance up to a very long leash and have me walk him the length of our driveway, while re-enforcing the commands he'd learned. He no longer yanked or pulled as had been his custom. Jan suggested carrying a tool belt filled with treats when we walked him. This would allow us to quickly reward Lance whenever he responded correctly to commands, thus combining exercise with training. During all these sessions, Lance was the picture of obedience.

When I told Jan about the aggressive and threatening behavior our dog had been demonstrating since moving in with us, she said, "Well, when a dog lives outside for that long a time, I guess you never really know what you're getting." While she cautioned us not to expect miracles, Jan recommended giving lots of verbal affirmations accompanied with occasional treats when Lance did the right thing. We were to offer only positive feedback, none of the negative variety. (Maybe I had misunderstood the alpha theory?) If he was acting in an unacceptable manner, we were to ignore our dog or even turn our backs on him, indicating our displeasure. Jan advised us not to stare at Lance, that intense eye contact from humans might intimidate him, provoking an aggressive reaction. She also suggested we learn to read his body language in order to anticipate his attacks. However, per Jan: "If he's actually lunging at either of you, or anyone else, you really should get rid of him. That kind of behavior is just unacceptable." *Hmm. I think he has already been doing that, and a bit* (pun intended) *more.*

Jan suggested that our dog might need a more intense level of treatment. At her recommendation, Clara and I, without Lance, visited a local sheep farm and dog training center that specializes in obedience training and is geared especially for herding breeds. Karen O'Brien, the owner, was a lady whose love for dogs was immediately obvious and I sensed with relief that we'd hit pay dirt. Lance's insanity was about to be corralled.

After outlining Lance's history to Karen, she rattled off a list of stressors that can cause uncontrollable aggressive behavior in a dog:

1. Physical punishment
2. Restricted movement
3. Boredom
4. Nothing to chew
5. Insufficient relaxation
6. Harassment from other animals/people
7. Inconsistent and/or no clear behavior guidelines taught to the dog
8. Lack of positive attention from owners
9. Insufficient mental or physical exercise
10. The dog sensing he has no capacity to ensure he will be well treated.

By my count, Lance had experienced at least nine of those mentioned, and on a continual basis, with number four being the possible exception.

Based on our description of his behavior, Karen ventured the educated guess that Lance was exhibiting defensive rage. The problem? He had become incapable of distinguishing between real and unreal threats. He defended himself by acting aggressively out of fear, even when there was no real danger to his well-being. This explanation of Lance's behavior was similar to the local vet's diagnosis. According to Karen, if a dog's aggressive behavior happens randomly and unpredictably, something has gone wrong with his wiring that training cannot fix. She said she'd have to actually meet Lance before making a final decision as to his trainability or lack thereof.

Karen declared Lance an unsuitable candidate for her herding classes. She doubted he would work well with the other dogs being trained on her farm, or with the trainers for that matter. She mentioned her aggressiveness rehabilitation program as a possible alternative. Correctly or not, I had already concluded from our conversation that Lance was in the "impaired wiring" category, which, by Karen's own definition, made him a bad fit for either of the programs. It wasn't so much a question of his intelligence level or even his advanced age that would impede his progress in her classes. He was simply too damaged, his aggressiveness too irrational to be corrected with training.

Before we left the farm, Karen gave us some words of encouragement. "I'm not saying your dog is a lost cause. I'm just saying that, as his owners, you're going to have to go the extra mile. If you can accept him as he is today, and might very well be for the rest of his life, you'll be giving him something he has never gotten up to now, but I have to warn you, he might not always show his appreciation."

Dejectedly, Clara and I walked through the parking lot to back to our car. I saw various canines, including several Border Collies, piling out of their owners' cars. The dogs rushed out onto a field, ready for training. There wasn't a non-wagging tail among them. No doubt years ago Lance would have been an A+ student in such a class. Now, this was just one more positive experience he'd miss out on.

We purchased some professionally recommended high-tech dog toys and artificial bones in the hopes they might help our dog relax. He showed no interest in any of them, even the ones we filled with cheese or peanut butter. I also tried to get him to retrieve balls and catch a Frisbee™.

No dice. He had the energy, but not the interest. This was yet another part of a younger dog's life that Lance would never know.

We concluded that even experts couldn't provide us with a foolproof plan that would straighten out our dog.

-17-

Broadening His Horizons

Expert opinions notwithstanding, we hung on to the belief that, if we were patient, with a little more time, our dog would calm down and adjust to his new owners. In the interim, we'd do our best to treat him as if he had always been ours.

One day during our first summer in Canadensis, Clara and I took Lance to a hiking spot called the Paulinskill Valley Trail, accessing it in Blairstown, New Jersey. This would be a major venture for Lance outside of the very small world he had lived in up to then. It would also be Clara's initial car ride with Lance. Being the good host, he generously treated her to his vehicular insanity.

The trip entailed a thirty-five-mile drive, so we firmly secured Lance in the car with the sturdiest—and most expensive, I might add—dog safety gate on the market. Lance knocked it down and was in the front seat harassing us before we even got out of the driveway. True to form, as we traveled, he kept up a steady stream of barking at each and every object outside the car that caught his attentive eye. After driving a half mile, and with Lance bouncing back and forth from Clara's lap to mine, I brought the car to a halt. We debated whether or not to continue the journey. To my surprise Clara, usually much less adventurous than I, was willing to forge ahead. She climbed over the front passenger seat, Lance happily following her. She leashed him and held on for dear life as I drove on. During the remainder of the trip, Clara and Lance engaged in a strenuous tug-of-war. Every once in a while, he lunged forward onto the front seat, pulling Clara off the back seat. Then, he'd revisit the backseat, graciously giving Clara the chance to sit down again. Not for long. Lance simply wouldn't stay put. His back-to-front-to-back darting and dashing was determined by whichever passing cars he felt needed his attention. Since Lance only went berserk in a car that was moving, I made several stops along the way just so that Clara could take a break from her wrestling match with the devil dog. A normal half-hour drive became an abnormal hour-and-fifteen-minute drive, thanks to Lance.

Finally, and to Clara's great relief, we arrived at the parking lot situated at the trail's start.

Because the opening to the path is heavily protected by large overhanging trees and other thick flora, when standing immediately outside the entrance it's impossible to see who or what might be about to exit from the trail. For this reason, we were taken by surprise when a white, curly-tailed, medium-sized, and unleashed dog came bolting out from the trail straight at us, followed by its panicky owners. Without provocation, the dog lunged at Lance. The situation was sticky because, although I didn't want an all-out dogfight, if I kept Lance restricted on his leash, he would be at a disadvantage defending himself. A brief melee ensued and it quickly became clear that the other dog wanted no further part of Lance. His owners corralled Oscar, a Samoyed, apologized to us and headed for their car.

That turned out to be the preliminary event.

After walking about a mile along the trail, we were met by a young girl on a rather large horse.

My guess is Lance had never seen an equine before in his life. He began circling it, barking at the top of his lungs, trying to control the horse's movements. We were fearful of our dog being trampled, but the rider seemed oblivious to what was going on. At first, that might have been understandable as her steed appeared unfazed by Lance's barking and lunging. Soon however, the horse began rearing up on its hind legs and then bringing its front legs back to the ground with tremendous force, landing dangerously close to Lance.

Clara and I both saw a disaster about to happen, but the rider, even though she was seated on a now obviously upset and agitated animal, continued chatting amiably with us ("Is your dog a Bernese?"). As politely as possible, I asked her to please continue her journey, but, not waiting for a response, I shouted "Pivot!" and prayed. To my great relief, as engrossed as Lance had been in corralling the horse, he turned around and rushed over to me. Clara and I took off with him down the trail. The horse's rider realized there was nobody left to talk to and proceeded on in the direction opposite of ours.

The rest of the hike was relaxing and unremarkable. The return trip in the car was just like any other ride with Lance—utter chaos. Clara did the driving while I attempted to restrain the frenzied canine next to me in the back seat. Being a bit stronger than Clara, we didn't have to make as many pit stops along way. Nonetheless, Lance gave me a good workout. By the time we got home, I felt like a cowboy who'd been struggling for hours to wrestle an ornery steer to the ground. Clara? She arrived home with sore arms and a determination never to ride in a car with Lance again.

-18-

Blunt Force Trauma

In Mount Bethel, Lance had received veterinary treatment only on an emergency basis until about age three and, after that, none until the incident that spurred his rescue. After taking him in, Clara and I decided to have him get a thorough physical checkup and any recommended inoculations. We already knew Lance was intermittently insane; we wanted to find out if he had any physical ailments that needed treatment.

Finances were tight at the time we rescued Lance, and several months passed before we were able to collect enough money to withstand a vet bill. We didn't get our dog to a doctor until fall of 2002. Clara, without going into the details of Lance's life, made the appointment over the phone.

On the way to the vet, Lance created his usual major disturbance in the car and then another one upon entering the clinic's waiting room. He lunged at every dog that got into his space, said "space" apparently being the entire waiting room. Something told me Lance was never going to be a dog-friendly dog. I dragged him to the most remote corner of the room, praying the leash would hold up until it was his turn to be seen. Thankfully, it did.

At last I was directed to walk him into a designated room and wait for a tech; Clara opted to remain in the waiting area. Once inside the room, Lance began pacing in circles. I tried to calm him, but my words fell on deaf (dog) ears.

A staff technician burst into the room with a cheery, "Hi Lance!"

Lance let out a throaty growl.

"Um...I'll be right back, sir."

Minutes later she returned with one of the vets. "Hello, Mr. Stoffel. I'm Dr. Chambers and this must be Lance. Does he always have trouble with checkups?"

"I don't know. This is the first time I've taken him for one."

"Really. And how old is he?"

"I'm guessing around ten heading for eleven."

"Hmm… interesting. Well, let's get him into the examination room."

With that, I handed Dr. Chambers the leash. The tech opened the door to the next room, but when the vet tried to escort Lance into it, the patient held his ground. The vet gave a slight tug on the leash; Lance growled.

Embarrassed and feeling like an inadequate pet owner, I apologized. "I don't know if this is going to work out. He's pretty much of a basket case. He goes after me too. I'm not sure I could help you much right now."

The doctor turned to his tech and said, "Get Randy and tell him to bring the muzzle. And get Joan too."

It took four of the staff, one being bitten in the process, to accomplish muzzling. After that, Lance, still in stubborn mode, had to be carried into an adjoining room to be examined, wrestling all the way with his handlers. As I went back out into the waiting area, I heard continued growling, only slightly muted by the muzzle. Within minutes, a vet came out and advised us that due to his unmanageability Lance could only be examined if he was sedated. We consented and he was anesthetized. As a result, the office visit lasted for more than four hours. When it was all over, Lance had gotten a physical exam and some preventative shots. He also had his blood drawn for testing purposes.

The examination over, one of the veterinarians (Dr. Chambers) came out to the waiting room and introduced himself to me. Clara had taken our car and gone shopping, one of her favorite pastimes.

"Mr. Stoffel, We need to talk. Please come with me."

The hospital bore his name so I figured Lance had just been treated by the best. After shaking hands, I followed Dr. Chambers down the hall to his office. He ushered me in.

"Make yourself comfortable."

I did, but not for very long.

"Don't you think it's a bit late in the game for this dog?"

"Yeah, he's getting up there. He'll be eleven by the end of the year."

"That's not what I'm talking about. I assume you're aware that your dog is absolutely loaded with scars. I mean from end to end. A lot of them look like bite marks, like he's been used for fighting. But there are others… What the hell happened here?"

"I didn't actually—

"In fact, it's so extensive some of the newer wounds actually overlap some of the older ones. I can't even separate… distinguish them all. In all my years, I'd say this is about the worst I've ever seen on an animal, at least on one that's still living. Frankly, I'm surprised he *is* still living. Were any of these wounds ever treated?"

"Oh, you're talking about the wrong dog. My dog's name is Lance and he's a Bord—"

"Yes, and he also has what I consider suspicious calcification in three ribs. Probably old fractures. This dog looks like a walking billboard for abuse. Why in the world would you suddenly decide to bring him here now?"

Something's wrong...

"Was this dog ever hit by a car?"

"I don't really know. I don't think so. He's been on a run pretty much all his life."

This makes no sense. He thinks he's talking about Lance but he can't be talking about Lance.

(With a mixture of sarcasm and disbelief) "You're not sure? Well, on top of everything else, at some point in his life, it looks like he suffered a fracture of the femur in his left hind leg. Presumably it was caused by some kind of blunt force trauma. How would *you* explain it?"

What's going on? He's telling me about some dog that's half-dead, not my dog. If Lance had been that beaten up, it would have been obvious. I couldn't be that clueless. I couldn't have missed it.

But maybe I did. Why would a vet lie? Oh my God! What a nightmare! We have a dog that isn't just psycho, to top it off he's a physical wreck and I didn't even see it. This whole thing is turning out to be some sort of a sick mess.

My reaction to the doctor's words: a painful combination of sorrow and anger. These feelings soon became mixed with a growing uneasiness. *Something more here than just a veterinarian talking to a dog owner. Something else is going on.* His dismissive tone gave me the feeling I was being lectured to. Here was a medical professional browbeating me, a layperson, to explain Lance's physical condition. Why?

Then, it hit me. *I'm under investigation. I'm being grilled.* What a perverse joke—on me. Just like Anna, I had allowed myself to get sucked into the Schmidts' twisted world. Lance was their handiwork, but I was the one being asked to account for his battered condition. There was something unreal about the whole thing. The irony may have been delicious, but I had no stomach for it.

Trying to keep my wits about me, I began outlining the details of Lance's life to Dr. Chambers, much as they had been outlined to me months ago by Anna. I was telling him the same strange story that had never fully made sense to me and hoping he would buy it. As I did, he occasionally jotted things down on a legal pad, "just for the record." *How very reassuring.* I insisted to Dr. Chambers that everything I was telling him, though hard to swallow, was factual. I presented my last line of defense: "But Dr. Chambers, think about it. Why would I bring a dog to you if I was the one that did all this damage to him? That would be pretty stupid. I'd be giving myself away. Plus, I'd be spending money on an animal I didn't even like."

Picturing myself being forced to testify under oath to someone somewhere, I prayed I made a credible witness on my own behalf.

The vet mulled over my comments and, without replying, moved on to the rest of his findings. I was afraid to keep listening.

Sounding only a bit less confrontational, he told me the dog he examined was also missing a chunk of the front of his tongue. Now I was sure we were talking about Lance. I had thought this deformity to be some kind of birth defect. The vet had a different opinion. He surmised that, due to the unique appearance of this particular damage, it may have been the result of a "negative encounter" with another animal. However, considering Lance's lifestyle, the litany of other unexplained injuries and the "irregular, jagged, and just unusual look" of this lesion, he would not rule out frostbite—or torture.

Lance had arthritis in one of his legs and throughout his spine. Additionally, he was suffering from spondylosis, which is, in simpler words, degeneration of the spine.

I knew I was listening to the results of a physical exam, but it sounded more and more like a coroner's report.

The veterinarian also discovered that Lance had considerable ligament damage (cause unknown) in his hind leg—the one that hadn't been broken. Dr. Chambers considered this injury no longer suitable for repair, ironically due to the unique combination of Lance's advanced age and his continuing high energy level. The vet felt that, besides the issue of being an older dog and thus slower to heal, his hyperactivity and aggressiveness would complicate the recovery process. I noticed that once in a while Lance favored this or that hind leg. He always quickly shook off the pain. Lance had learned to live with his injuries—all of them.

Blood analysis showed Lance testing positive for Lyme disease which, among many other symptoms, can cause severe joint pain and inflamed nerves. Who knows how long he had been infected and gone untreated?

Lance tipped the scales at a hefty sixty-eight pounds, a heavier-than-average weight for his breed. No doubt this was the combined result of Anna's home cooking and years of insufficient exercise.

Based on the vet's report, Lance was actually in better physical condition than might have been expected—he was still alive. He'd completely fooled me. I considered him the picture of health. Visualizing him breaking off that brand-new run back in Mount Bethel or on one of our grueling hikes, I could not figure out for the life of me how a dog that had endured so much physical damage could still have so much strength and stamina.

This visit to the vet was not without a few, small silver linings. In spite of having lived outside all his life and no baths, he was currently flea, mite, and tick-free and sporting a healthy odor-free coat. Another plus: his weatherworn collar was safely replaced with a new one while he had been sedated, something Clara or I would never have dared to do.

The conversation (or was it an inquisition?) over, I escaped the interrogation room and went back out to the waiting room. I sat there, kicking myself mentally for never completely putting two and two together during all that time in Mount Bethel. Until 2001, I had never met people like the Schmidts and, naively, would have found it hard to believe their kind existed. Maybe that's why I didn't immediately recognize them for what they were.

Ten minutes passed, then ten more. A desk person said Lance was still recuperating from his sedation. *I suppose so or could the staff possibly be taking Lance into protective custody and calling legal authorities?*

Eventually that train of thought was happily broken when I spotted a black and white tornado heading towards me, pulling a vet tech with him. He was a handful, even though woozy from sedation. Reaching me, he attempted a few of his dance moves, looking much like a drunken sailor. There was no doubt he was glad to see me. Apparently, *he* didn't think I was such a bad owner.

Prior to leaving, I made the next appointment almost out of self-defense, wanting to give the strongest impression possible that I was a responsible dog owner.

Exiting the hospital, the words "blunt force trauma" continued whirling around in my mind with a vengeance. How could I have not picked up on such massive physical damage? It never once occurred to me to give Lance a thorough onceover. His strength and energy had completely fooled me and, of course, he wouldn't have let me examine him anyway.

As I opened my car door I looked down at Lance.

"Hey buddy…"

I got his attention.

"What did those Schmidt bastards do to you?"

He gave me a quick, nervous, half-wag of his tail and then jumped into the car, his way of saying *Can we drop the subject and go home now?* Inside Lance lay a collection of dark tales that would never be told.

Because of this exam, I now knew, in graphic detail, the physical damage Lance had suffered. It was much more horrible than anything I imagined. His life had been the very definition of pure hell.

The bottom fell out of my already low opinion of the Schmidts. Obviously, strapping firecrackers to this dog had not been some isolated act of depravity. Their maltreatment and neglect of this dog could now only be described as purposeful, methodical and continual. Months ago, the words quirky, bizarre, and neglectful had become insufficient to describe the Schmidts; now even calling them malicious would be too kind. I had to force myself to quit the ugly word search I was conducting to perfectly describe them. It was only hurting me.

Dr. Chamber's findings stirred feelings in me no pet owner should be forced to deal with. I was overwhelmed with what could only be described as disheartened outrage. As a therapist, I am always encouraging clients to accept and let go of this or that negative aspect of their life. The catch is, when taking that approach to its extreme, one might start trying to see nothing as unacceptable. Getting too philosophical? I guess what I'm trying to say is that maybe it's best to accept that not one second of Lance's life under the Schmidt regime could ever be undone and maybe it's also best to admit that being continually angry at the Schmidts would do no good. I know I'll never, never accept what they put this dog through. Though there are a lot more moral gray areas in my life than there used to be, abuse of a dog will never be one of them. Not ever.

Since there was nothing that could be done to treat the mountain of damage that had been done to Lance, I decided to leave the more gruesome information in Dr. Chambers' report out of the report Clara would receive from me. One disheartened dog owner was enough.

Do I dare say Lance was a "lucky dog"? In some warped sense he was, although his was a grim luck to be sure. It was now patently obvious that there were so many different ways he could have already died: from abuse at the hands of humans, fights he had with other animals, eating rancid food, living outside during periods of excessive heat or cold, or not getting any medical care for the greater part of a decade. Yet, defying all logic, here he was still standing. The same fate that had forced him to endure ten gruesome years allowed him to come out a survivor, damaged to be sure, but a survivor nonetheless. Until today, I had been impressed by this older dog's stamina. Now I was amazed—and grateful—he was even breathing.

The closest I'd ever come to an explanation for Lance's mental condition was provided by Dr. Chambers' description of his physical condition. The kind of life he was forced to live made his behavior, though unpredictable, upsetting and, at times, frightening, at least more under-standable. I made a mental note beginning from that day on: Whenever he acted out, I'd recollect the details in today's exam in order to remind me where my dog had been and where he was coming from. If I ever found myself losing patience with Lance and ready to give up on him, I'd remember those three grisly words—blunt force trauma.

-19-

Aftercare

The veterinary examination provided graphic details of the damage done. The vet discovered many of Lance's injuries, but was uncertain of their exact causes. It's probably just as well. What purpose would it serve to know the details? Lance had lived a horror show, case closed. For whatever reason, Anna had understated just how miserable this dog's life had been. Looking for a silver lining in all this mess, I found one. Lance had gotten out of Mount Bethel just in time. It was now clear that the conversation I had overheard between Jack Schmidt and his son about killing their dog was very likely more than idle, dark humor. Lance was a hell of a survivor, but I think even his luck had been about to run out.

While sad and angry over Lance's physical condition, my admiration for him was growing. The vet expressed amazement Lance still had a pulse. This dog was a real die-hard.

Two questions continued to haunt me. How could I have lived so close to an abused dog for so long and not realized what was going on? Then, when I started to walk him, why did I not immediately sense the gravity of the situation? I'm still searching for the answers.

Nothing much could be done about Lance's death-warmed-over medical condition. He would have to keep living with most of his ailments as he had been up to now.

For the Lyme disease, the vet prescribed an oral antibiotic. Neither Clara nor I felt brave enough to attempt shoving a pill down his throat by hand. The solution? We wrapped his medication in liverwurst and placed it on the floor. Quite often, he'd manage to ingest the liverwurst while spitting out the pill. A second, third, or even fourth attempt would be required. Who knows? Maybe Lance realized that if he kept spitting out the pill, he'd keep getting more liverwurst.

Lance frustrated all our efforts at preventing insect infestation. We dared not attempt putting on a tick and flea collar, nor would he allow us to apply anti-insect ointment or powder, or brush him. Yet, despite his lack of cooperation and very thick coat, he lived his entire life with us virtually insect-free. Did he strike fear in bugs, too?

All the trips Lance ever took to the vet proved to be highly problematic. Of course, there were the chaotic car rides. In addition, Lance was always a huge behavioral issue inside the animal hospital. Whenever he entered the waiting room, all hell broke loose. Lance wasn't simply curious about the other animals there, he wanted at them.

Following that first visit and per the vet's recommendation, we gave Lance ten milligrams of calming Valium before any visit. The medication didn't faze him in the slightest. Consequently, on all of his subsequent trips to the veterinarian, he had to be muzzled and professionally sedated even for a basic examination. I was learning that, when it came to Lance, nothing was easy.

On follow-up appointments, in order to keep the peace, I didn't bring Lance inside immediately upon arrival. Instead, I called from the parking lot to let the receptionist know we were on the premises. She, in turn, would call me back when it was Lance's turn to be seen. This minimized his physical presence in the hospital. When we entered, the staff would inevitably be wearing that *Oh no, that dog is here!* look. Every time we exited, I swear I could hear a voice on a loudspeaker announcing the "all clear" alert: "Attention staff, the emergency is over. Lance has left the building."

During his last scheduled visit to Chambers Animal Hospital, Lance—Valium and all—would not allow anyone to muzzle him. Just about the entire work force, including some front desk people, made an unsuccessful stab at getting him to cooperate. One employee was bitten, or was it two? No longer up to dealing with Lance and his issues, the staff at the Chambers Animal Hospital threw up their hands in collective surrender, declaring Lance too unmanageable to be treated. We were unceremoniously discharged—something to do with concern over staff and visitor safety. Adding financial insult to injury, even though Lance hadn't received treatment on that final visit, I got a bill for "unsuccessful muzzling attempts."

We had to find a new vet, which suited me just fine. Due to Lance's sad physical condition, I always felt I was being held under a cloud of suspicion by all of Dr. Chambers' personnel. But, where to go with Lance for medical treatment?

Next up—the Cresco Veterinary Clinic. It was much closer to home, making the strenuous ride with Lance shorter, if not sweeter. However, it had a drawback of its own. The waiting room was extremely small, a fact I unfortunately didn't become aware of until we made our first—and last—visit there.

Upon entering, Lance lunged at several dogs sitting nearby, upsetting their owners and setting off a chorus of snarls and whimpers among the dogs in Lance's crosshairs. As the other dog owners struggled to restrain their pets, I did an immediate U-turn, dragging Lance back outside. From there, I called the receptionist so we could coordinate a less dramatic entrance. Fifteen minutes later, I got the signal to proceed back inside. As planned, the door to the examination room was already open so I quickly ushered Lance into it, before he could reintroduce himself to those in the waiting room.

Different clinic, same Lance. After a lengthy wrestling match with the staff, Lance had to be muzzled and anesthetized for an ear cleaning. Although this visit was more successful than our last one to Chambers, we worried about the continual anesthetization of our dog for even the slightest medical procedure. As luck would have it, Gina, my stepdaughter, came to the rescue. She had a non-biting, but totally unruly dog that was being cared for successfully by a traveling vet the locals called Dr. Doolittle. He was considered a miracle worker with hard-to-handle cases, many of which were referred to him by animal hospitals in the area. His name: McKinley Gordon.

On the phone, I gave Dr. Gordon details of Lance's violent history, aggressiveness, and resistance to medical treatment. Despite this heads up and the fact that seeing Lance would require a fifty-five-mile round-trip on his part, he set up an appointment. Prior to Dr. Gordon's first visit to our home, I put Lance out in the yard as the vet had requested. The doctor reasoned his initial meeting with our dog might be less stressful if he was already sitting down in the living room when Lance came back inside.

While waiting for the doctor to arrive on the day of his first visit, Clara expressed her misgivings. "You know, Tasha (Gina's dog) isn't really at all like Lance. For one thing, he's not psychotic."

"I was thinking pretty much the same thing. I wonder if this guy knows what he's getting into. Hey, and what are we getting into? You know, what's our liability? Are we off the hook because he's a vet?" I pictured the bloodbath that would soon be taking place on our property.

The clatter of a badly worn muffler on an even more badly worn vehicle announced Dr. Gordon's arrival as he pulled into our driveway. Seeing him, Lance let loose a serenade of unfriendly, high-decibel barks from the side yard that followed the doctor right up to our front door.

Dr. Gordon, sporting a shock of white hair and a grandfatherly disposition, looked to be somewhere in his late sixties. He was a throwback. For one thing, he made house calls, which immediately eliminated those exhausting and unnerving car trips. For another, he did not engage in what he considered excessive and needless testing of an animal, especially a dog of Lance's advanced years. His fees were low, so ridiculously low I got the feeling he still worked at his trade more for his love of animals than for the money. Most importantly, it quickly became clear that he knew how to conduct himself around Lance, respecting his volatility without showing fear. As a result, veterinary care became a much less eventful experience.

Over the years, the good doctor had developed his own techniques for dealing with dangerous dogs, "stuff they don't teach you in school." During that first meeting and all subsequent visits, Lance was allowed inside only after Dr. Gordon had seated himself in the same spot on the living room sofa. "Dogs like predictability, stability. My guess: probably too much commotion for him at the animal hospitals—you know, all the people and animals. At least here he's on his home turf." Lance always rushed in from outside, making a threatening beeline for the doctor. Nothing ever happened. He'd content himself with thoroughly sniffing his potential prey. During the first house call, Dr. Gordon rated a few half-hearted growls; on subsequent visits, none. The bloodshed Clara and I had anticipated never materialized. We were amazed by our dog's inexplicable tolerance for someone who—by Lance's own logic—was both a stranger and an intruder.

In our dog's presence, this vet never used the name Lance. "He's probably not very fond of that name. Why push his buttons?" Instead, he opted to employ one of my favorite made-up nicknames for our dog. I got a kick out of hearing a seasoned medical professional address his patient as "Poopinski."

McKinley Gordon was all business around Lance. He never touched or even approached our dog except for a medical purpose. Despite his well-earned reputation, the doctor harbored no illusions about ever befriending Lance. "It's a little late for that. He lived too long in the wilds. I know my limits when I see 'em."

Dr. Gordon never once insinuated we were crazy for putting up with such an unstable animal. He referred to Lance as a dog "with some quirks and issues, but hey, we all have 'em."

Per the doctor: "From what you've been telling me, it sounds like this fella's been to hell and back. Darnedest thing. Looking at him, you'd never guess it. Banged up and all, he acts like a dog half his age. Very alert. Lots of energy. Let's see if we can keep 'im going."

Dr. Gordon devised a unique method for administering any needed injections. With Lance standing on all fours, I'd straddle his back with my legs while keeping a firm grip on his collar, all the while praising him verbally. Dr. Gordon would then sneak up from behind and inject Lance in his rump. Although I was less than enthused about my role in the procedure, this vet was so adept he got the job done before Lance could even begin to think about snapping at me. We utilized this tactic on several occasions with great success, no muzzle or sedative needed. Sometimes old school trumps new school.

Chambers Animal Hospital, with its posh building, state-of-the-art medical equipment, large workforce, banks of computers, and extensive retail sales operation, was far less impressive to me than Dr. Gordon, with his '80s Chevy van and weather-beaten medical bag. Except for any emergency, he would forever be our vet of choice.

Excerpts from Lance's Medical Records
(*Chambers Animal Hospital*)

"Owner gave Diazepam 5 mg (10 tablets) one
hour ago to sedate for exam and workup…"

"…Muzzled for exam…Chronic history
of intermittent lameness…"

"…Very tense. Was good with muzzle until
mat near ear was clipped. Then growled…"

"…Two weeks ago Lance ate woodchuck.
Developed diarrhea…"

"…Owners not able to treat topically the
hotspot b/c dog will attack them…"

"…Not a good candidate for ACL surgery. Not
able to touch dog and very hard to muzzle…"

"…Still not able to apply anything topically
on dog (bites owner)…"

"…Limps on hind end and gives aspirin on those
days (about once a week)…

DIAGNOSTICS: Muzzled but dog flipped out.

ASSESSMENT: not able to fully examine, has
been treated for lyme disease, owners not able
to apply frontline…

…Gave Diazepam tabs for sedation/phobias…"

-20-

Shell Shock

Based on his medical report, by all rights our nutjob of a dog should have been perched on death's doorstep. The dog joining me on humongous walks presented a very different picture. Only time would tell just how much life Lance had left in him.

In the meantime, we continued living with him and all his "quirks," as Dr. Gordon called them. One was an inability to handle loud noises. Just days after moving into our new home, it rained cats and dogs (sorry, couldn't help myself). The first few cracks of thunder got Lance's attention; after several more, he was a changed dog. Bug-eyed with fear, he began a frantic search for cover, first making an unsuccessful attempt to squeeze under the sofa, then hiding under the kitchen table by knocking chairs out of the way. He hadn't escaped the noise so the search for safety branched out. Howling and whining, Lance bolted from room to room, fruitlessly seeking relief. He wound up in our bedroom and, scraping feverishly with his paws, tried to worm his way under a bed that had no clearance. Frustrated, he scooted into the corner trying to burrow under the lamp table, sending Clara's favorite lamp crashing to the floor in pieces.

Fighting fire with fire, I turned on the television and CD player full blast, leaving them on during the all-night storm. Other than an unusually loud crack of thunder here and there, Lance was distracted by the electronic noise. Unfortunately, so were Clara and I. Two very exhausted dog owners rose in the morning. Lance, on the other hand, had slept like a lamb.

There was also the matter of fireworks set off during the days surrounding every Fourth of July and New Year's Day. The explosions instantly sent Lance darting from room to room in a futile attempt to escape the sound shocks. Again, I utilized the CD player and TV, sometimes cranking up the air conditioners for good measure. We developed our own tradition for celebrating Fourths of July and New Year's: inside our house, we endured a steady, earsplitting racket that distracted Lance from the intermittent explosions coming from outside.

Such was the case, except for one particular evening, just before that year's Independence Day. Clara and I had gone out to watch a local fireworks display. We returned home to find a total mess. Chairs overturned, lamps lying on the floor, racks of DVDs and CDs toppled over—it looked like our house had been through an earthquake, or a burglary, and, even worse, our dog was nowhere in sight. Outside we went, calling for Lance, at the same time trying to figure how in the world he'd gotten out of the house. Our calls went unanswered. Lance was not to be found. Now we were sick with worry. *Who did this? Did they let Lance loose? Did they hurt him?*

Back inside, we conducted another search and found Lance cowering in the darkest corner of our bedroom. Earlier that night, I had forgotten to sound proof the house before leaving, and our dog reacted to fireworks in his typically desperate manner. Never again did we leave him alone during a Fourth of July weekend or New Year's Eve.

Lance also could not handle the noise made by firearms. It just so happened that our house sat near thousands of acres of game lands. We dreaded the start of every hunting season as it meant having to deal with our dog's pained reaction to every gunshot day in, day out for several months. During the off-season, gun owners showed no mercy on Lance, sporadically taking target practice in the woods nearby.

How did Lance deal with thunder, gunfire, and firecrackers all those years when he was stuck outside? I know that Anna couldn't have always been there trying to at least console him. When she couldn't, Lance was stuck, completely isolated, in a horrendous state of pain and panic from which there was no escape.

Under House Arrest

The first winter after rescuing Lance, Clara and I took a brief vacation out of town, a respite from work and the devil dog. Based on several recommendations, we selected a boarding kennel located in Stroudsburg.

Clara gave the manager a heads up. "He's a fear biter."

"Don't worry. We've handled dogs like that."

"Oh, really? We were concerned about that."

"Yup. They always settle down."

On the way to the airport, we dropped Lance off at his temporary residence. The kennel was clean and airy, the staff very courteous. I led Lance to his decent-sized cage in which fresh food and water were already waiting for him. All in all, a very professional setup.

Five days later we returned to retrieve our dog, just in time as it turned out. We were met by a distraught and apologetic staff. Despite all their efforts, Lance had drunk little water and eaten no food in our absence. He let no one in to clean his cage or to leash him up for a walk. In fact, he hadn't let anyone near him, period. Having had no phone number to contact us, the staff had been in a quandary as to how to keep him alive.

I headed with an employee towards Lance's cage, dreading what I'd find. There he was, surrounded by his own feces and looking weather-beaten. Undernourished and dehydrated, he still had the energy to give me an enthusiastic greeting, one I wasn't sure I deserved. When I brought him out to the car where Clara was waiting, she took one look at his ragged condition and angrily exclaimed, "What did they do to him?" I explained to her he did it to himself. Oh, the guilt. Scratch boarding.

Had that vacation gone on any longer, Lance would have starved himself to death. The dog that terrorized us couldn't live without us.

During the following fall, Anna volunteered to take in Lance while we traveled to Maryland for our son's wedding. Thank God! Imagine the countless moving violations I would have gotten driving all the way to Maryland and back with our dog in the car. Not that Clara would have permitted such a journey anyway.

The day before we left for Maryland, I drove Lance to Anna's home. She ushered us both into her first-floor den. While I waited there, Anna took Lance upstairs, hoping to familiarize him with his temporary surroundings. This was Lance's second visit to Anna's house. Many years earlier, he had made that unsuccessful first attempt that lasted only minutes.

Just as I plopped myself onto a couch, I heard a growl quickly followed with an "Ow!" Anna came back down the basement stairs, leading the devil dog. He'd just bitten her husband. I envisioned my trip to Maryland evaporating. Surprisingly, Anna advised me not to worry and to enjoy the wedding. She insisted on keeping Lance.

When I returned a week later, Anna told me that during our time away, she had lived with our dog in the basement while her husband stayed upstairs. After thanking Anna profusely for her patience and her husband's (did he have a choice?), I took my leave with Lance.

Before going back home, we took a brief stroll around Lance's old neighborhood. Most likely, he didn't get too nostalgic. As we walked, Lance occasionally turned to look at me, wearing a disappointed and reprimanding look. *Why did you leave me for so many days? Are you really trustworthy? How could you do this to me?* More guilt.

As a result of these two far-from-successful dog-sitting attempts, Clara and I concluded we could not, in good conscience, ask anyone else to care for our dog. We also couldn't have Lance traveling in the car with us. Clara remained dead set against getting into any Lance-occupied vehicle. She was afraid that his unruliness would ultimately lead to a car accident and I couldn't debate her logic. Following that trip to Maryland, we would be restricted to rare day trips for as long as we were to have Lance. We had become both owners and prisoners of a dog.

-22-

Life or Death?

The unsettled and unsettling dog that revealed himself the moment he moved into 21 Oak Tree Drive was the dog we continued to struggle living with.

There is a slogan in the recovery field: "Live life on life's terms." It refers to accepting and dealing with whatever fate throws at you, rather than spending your days filled with regrets and fruitless attempts at changing the unchangeable, or turning to drugs and alcohol to self-medicate. Hard work indeed. In our home, living life on life's terms meant Lance's terms, also hard work. He hadn't changed, but Clara and I had. Both of us developed a more heightened awareness and alertness, a sixth sense, in an effort to lessen the frequency of Lance's attacks. We became better skilled at not doing things to agitate him, primarily by keeping our distance. That said, there were still plenty of times that our dog, apparently self-agitated, caught us off guard. He had never actually drawn blood from me. Every time he snapped at me, I managed to yank my hand away just as his jaw was closing in for the kill. Clara was not so lucky. For her, Lance reserved attacks too unforeseen and illogical to be anticipated.

Once, Clara was in the kitchen offering our dog a treat. She bent down and put out her hands, one empty and one holding a piece of cheese. Lance, visibly flustered, quickly looked back and forth at her two hands and then, instead of taking the treat, leapt up at Clara, biting her in the face; she still carries a sizable scar above her upper lip.

On another occasion, while Clara was out walking with Lance in our neighborhood, a child sped past on a bicycle at the exact moment a broken tree branch happened to fall onto the road. This combination of events unnerved our dog and, without warning, he lunged at Clara and bit her calf. A tree limb snapped and so had Lance. She scolded him. "What the hell is wrong with you? That's the end of your walk." Back home they marched, Clara warning him along the way to "start getting your act together." Once inside, she cleaned off her bloody mess of a wound, purposely ignoring Lance as Jan Bittner had suggested we do when disappointed with his behavior. Occasionally peeking at him, Clara saw he was wearing that apologetic expression he so often did after one of these incidents.

I teased Clara and told her our dog would never be able to puncture my skin like he did hers, because my reflexes were superior. My attempt at humor failed to impress her.

In fact, this attack on Clara while they were walking brought us to a crossroads with Lance, even if we couldn't explain that to him. At this juncture—early 2004—we had been living with Lance for over a year and a half. We were trying to treat our dog the way he deserved to be treated, but sometimes he wouldn't let us. Neither of us had become totally adept at gauging his mood and his volatility was showing no signs of disappearing. Inside the house, we were never sufficiently at ease to fully enjoy any kind of interaction with our dog. We had to make a decision, one based on the feeling that the kind of Lance we had now, might very well be the only kind of Lance we would ever have. Did we want to keep living like this? We were told by experts and laypersons alike that he was damaged beyond repair. We were coming to the same conclusion.

Keeping him, but permanently relegating him to our backyard, was out of the question. He would be right back in the situation he'd been saved from.

Our remaining choices? Pull off a miracle and find a more suitable home for Lance, have him euthanized, or resign ourselves to the status quo.

Months earlier, up to here with his behavior, Clara had called the Border Collie Rescue Association to inquire if there might be a more suitable placement for Lance than us. She was informed that organization could not take on the responsibility of finding another home for such an unstable dog. The association's representative told Clara that "dogs like that are usually put down."

Out of desperation, Clara contacted the same organization a second time, hoping and praying a dog rescue organization would rescue us from the dog we had rescued. Since Lance's behavior hadn't changed, the association wouldn't change its stance. At that moment, Lance was officially placed in the lost cause category by an organization that specializes in rescuing dogs of his breed. Lance was a canine hot potato that no one else wanted any part of.

Based on our experience boarding him in a kennel, we knew that if we gave him to the local shelter, he would either starve himself to death or be euthanized.

Who in their right mind would take Lance? Would I have, if he'd shown his "flip" side while still in Mount Bethel? In good conscience, we would have to make full disclosure to anyone thinking of taking our headache. I was certain if this dog left our home, he was as good as dead; we'd just be temporarily postponing the execution, dumping our problem on someone else who'd be forced to pull the switch.

We were the last stop for Lance. He had survived more than a decade of abuse and neglect before finally being given the chance at a better life. He was blowing his one and only opportunity.

Clara was deathly afraid of Lance. Admittedly, at times I was fearful, too. We had an uncomfortable conversation. With nowhere to send him, it revolved around having Lance destroyed.

Not knowing what else to do, I searched "reasons for euthanizing a dog" on my computer. I braced myself for a gruesome journey.

Entering the world of electronic fact and fiction, I didn't stay long, just enough to pick up on a few recurring themes:

Some people on the Internet argued that being in physically decrepit condition was sufficient reason to put a dog down. According to his medical report, that would be Lance. In reality, no way! This dog was an ageless wonder. He carried his beaten body extremely well. Our dog might at times have acted brain-damaged, but he wasn't brain-dead.

Others favored euthanasia if the dog's quality of life was sufficiently poor and not likely to get better. By that measure, Lance might have been a prime candidate for extermination throughout the first ten years of his life. The sad fact is dogs are regularly destroyed because others have mangled them beyond repair. Happily, our dog no longer qualified using this criterion. Lance had managed to live long enough to finally get treated like a normal dog, even if he no longer was one.

Another group of respondents insisted that euthanasia was the answer for a mentally ill dog:

"These dogs can't possibly have any quality of life, they are always on edge."

"Biters need killing! Period. There are millions of good dogs, *don't waste oxygen on nutcases.*"

"I'm sure there are some dogs that are permanently mentally

imbalanced. They will never be trustworthy. A dog like that has no purpose, and should be put down."

"Should a dog be destroyed if it can't be trusted? I love dogs but 'Yes' is the answer."

"If a dog is born messed up, there's nothing you can do about it. These dogs can't be fixed."

"If you have a dog for more than a year and he is not improving, there is no hope."

"If a dog can't even be trusted by the owner, what's the point? That dog is a lawsuit waiting to happen. The dog needs to be nuked."

"Exterminate for your sake and the dog's. A psychotic dog like that would be much happier being humanely euthanized."

"It's only a dog, for God's sake."

In less than ten minutes, my search on the Internet ended. The topic generated too many depressing comments. I reminded myself these were just opinions. Did Lance have a few diagnosable disorders? Probably. Do we routinely euthanize mentally ill humans? No.

Shouldn't Lance have some say in this? Did he want to be put out of his misery? When attempting to determine if a person has suicidal tendencies, one of the diagnostic criteria is their degree of future orientation. How much or how little interest do they show in pursuing productive activities today and thereafter? Applying that criteria to our dog, it became clear Lance was very future-oriented. As soon as we finished one walk, he was already gearing up for the next one. On those treks, he cavorted like a youngster. This was a dog burying bones all around the backyard, saving for a rainy day. He always situated himself strategically in order to watch Clara when she was in the kitchen cooking; he knew something tasty was in the works. Were any of these the behaviors of a dog ready to pack it in?

Happily parading around the house with a treat before devouring it, looking the picture of contentment lying by the fireplace on a cold winter's night, bringing me one of my sneakers as his way of letting me know we were going for a hike—Lance was getting a chance for the first time in his life to live a dog's life. Why cut all of that short?

Clara and I had a heart-to-heart about Lance, who was with us in the living room, stretched out on his pillow, oblivious to the fact that his life was up for grabs again (Or was he? You just never know with those Border Collies).

I rarely make decisions, tending to let others' decisions make me. This time was different. I was prepared to advocate for Lance's life, all because of a phrase I will never forget: blunt force trauma. However, my wife was getting it the worst from Lance, so I knew the decision would ultimately be hers. I could only plead for just a little more patience on her part.

"Babes, I know he's got you terrified. I'll never second-guess your decision. I just can't help but think we'd be having him put down just when he was about to straighten out."

Proving to be as much a softy as I, Clara responded, "Well, let's give him a little bit more time, and see if he starts to get it. But he better start getting it pretty soon." I was more than willing to go along with her plan. We both hopped back onto the optimism train.

People asked us why we'd keep a dog like Lance. Clara and I both knew that, if we didn't, that would be the end of the line for him. We were living with a dog that had defied death too many times to count. Having miraculously survived so many horrid years and been snatched from the jaws of death only to be killed by his rescuers—that would have been an unconscionable cruelty, a twisted form of abuse in itself.

Living day in and day out with a damaged dog, it eventually became pointless to concern ourselves with who abused him, all the details of how and the injustice of it all. We didn't need to delve deeper into his past, its consequences were right in front of us. Now all that mattered was how Clara and I, not his previous owners, were treating him. He was our dog and therefore our responsibility, nobody else's. If other people had been living with us at the time, our decision would have been infinitely more difficult. Since that was not the case, we agreed to do our best to put up with Lance for the duration of whatever life he had left, knowing full well what his fate would be if we didn't.

This dog would live to see another day and maybe a few more after that. Surviving is what the "die-hard" did best and he had just done it again. We were in the presence of the first *dog* with nine lives.

–23–

Petting Protocol

For the time being, Lance was safe. He would remain so until the day came when Clara or I said "Enough is enough!" Since our dog wasn't going anywhere, we had to figure out how to better deal with his tension-provoking behavior.

Clara gave Lance an ultimatum: "Listen, you ungrateful cur, if you bite me again you are gone! This is your absolute last chance!" Did he understand English? The fact is, although he continued to threaten her, he never bit Clara again. Of course, their chat didn't dissuade him from going after others, me included. Maybe I should have had a similar conversation with Lance.

In an attempt to foster Lance's trust in her, Clara developed a gutsy and unique procedure. Keeping her hands behind her, she held food with her mouth, letting Lance take it with his teeth. At first, she used very long bread rolls. As she gained confidence, Clara gradually decreased the length of whatever morsel she offered him. While Lance had once bitten Clara's face when she was feeding him by hand, he never bit Clara's face when *it* was feeding him. I never attempted to imitate this trick of hers. I didn't have the nerve to.

There's another phrase utilized in Twelve-step programs: Act "as if." Its significance? Even if you are not yet the person you want to be, if you keep thinking and acting like the person you want to become, eventually you'll succeed. It's a little like "fake it till you make it."

In a variation of that theme, we decided to act as if Lance were a normal dog. We had spent months mostly steering clear of him in the house. We switched gears and pretended Lance was your garden variety dog. We hoped that if the environment around Lance was treating him as if he were okay, he might just start feeling he was. We'd have to fake it until Lance could make it.

Normal dogs get petted. However, if we were going to pet our dog as part of this "normalcy" thing, we had to take some precautions. If touching Lance was never to be truly safe, we could at least try to make it less risky.

Petting Lance unannounced tended to startle him, and, at times, led to snarls and snaps. At first, we decided to only touch him if he seemed to be indicating a wish to be petted. That way, we figured the chances were better he'd react more appropriately. Like any self-respecting dog, he'd occasionally present himself in front of one of us, tail happily wagging, and look up as if to say *Okay, you can start petting me now.* We often didn't have the courage to oblige. Those times we did, Lance was always a threat to attack even though he was the one that initiated the interaction. To further complicate matters, sometimes he wouldn't growl before an attack, depriving us of the benefit of that early warning sign. When it came to the devil dog, appearances could be so deceiving.

As we got braver, Clara or I might beckon our dog to come and get some hands-on affection. Since neither of us was ever sure what kind of mood Lance was in, every visit from him, solicited or unsolicited, provoked tension.

Sometimes, Lance flinched before even being touched, a warning to go no further, that he was about to lose it. I also developed the ability to sense an impending attack by watching Lance's face intently. If he took on a certain look, I'd yank my hand away, leaving him snapping at air. There were other occasions when, startled by our attempted positive physical contact, he'd quickly distance himself from us. For Lance it was fight or flight.

Over time, and with Lance's "fangs on" instruction, Clara and I developed somewhat safer petting techniques. We learned what was acceptable and unacceptable by trial and error, our dog letting us know when we got it wrong.

Lance was not to be touched absent-mindedly, or without having his mouth in one's range of vision, or for more than a few seconds. We learned to pet Lance only when facing him, thereby lessening the chance he would be spooked; attempting to pet Lance from behind was foolhardy. If he was seated facing me, I could touch him on his face alongside his eyes. Petting under his chin, on the nape, or his back was riskier. It was always dangerous to pet Lance if he was seated or standing at my side with both of us facing in the same direction.

Rubbing him with one's foot was totally out. Lance taught me that. Following one of our more grueling walks, Lance lay down in front of my recliner after I had collapsed into it. I began gently touching him with my foot, but not for long. I still have that foot, thanks to the fact I had on hiking boots when Lance attacked.

We quickly learned that Lance was never to be petted if he was lying down. Usually, we just talked to him when he assumed any kind of prone position. Even if he lay on his back exposing his stomach to be rubbed, there was no guarantee he would not snap and a good likelihood he would.

Yet, if he was in that same belly-up position, he'd allow me to grab his front paws and pump them forwards and backwards. Frequently, after such play, Lance would leap up and do his Aztec Side-step dance out of sheer joy. He took great delight in this game. Often he'd lie down on his back, belly-up, with his legs extended "asking" me to hold his paws. Of course, since he was in the dreaded lying position, I couldn't help but worry he might be trying to set me up. You just never knew which Lance you were going to get at any given moment. I'm not even sure Lance knew which Lance *he'd* be getting.

Talk about asking for trouble. I don't know what I was thinking (or if I even was) but one day I began alternately running the palms of my hands down the front of Lance's face from the top of his head to the end of his snout. Immediately his tail started wagging, so this technique stayed in the petting protocol. Although my hands passed right over his mouth (of course, I was on high alert!) and therefore were easy targets, I never got any negative feedback from him. Why? It defies explanation.

Alertness and quick reflexes were essential when letting one's hand enter Lance's biting zone. Whenever I pulled my hand away from him just as he snapped at me, I congratulated myself for being one step ahead of him. The truth was, in spite of our best efforts, neither of us ever fully perfected the ability to read Lance and predict his outbursts. When he approached, we never knew who was coming, Dr. Jekyll or Mr. Hyde. All we could do was hope for the best. In many situations we either gave him a quick pat of the hand, followed by an even quicker retreat of that hand, or, a safer option, just some verbal praise without touching him at all. Quite often, Lance might be looking to be petted but, because of our fears, he had to settle for kind words.

The first night Lance invited himself to bed with us we just held our breath, didn't say "Boo" and lay still. We both spent the night sleeping with one eye open.

Eventually having him on the bed became less fear-provoking, only because we learned the rules: do not touch him when he was in the bed (whether you also were or not), never get out of a Lance-occupied bed in the dark, and never get into bed if he was already there. In the latter situation, we had to call Lance out into the living room and then rush into bed before he realized what was going on. Invariably, if we left the bedroom door open, he'd come running back into the bedroom and take a flying leap up onto the bed to join us. If we went into the bedroom and closed the door before Lance had entered, he respected our need for privacy and spent the night on his doggie bed in the living room.

Acting "as if" could only be carried so far. There were situations when just going near our dog was out of the question, let alone petting him. For reasons known only to him, Lance would sometimes scurry to the corner of whatever room he was in and take a position lying firmly pressed against a wall. His body telegraphed self-protectiveness, his face fear-stricken panic. It hurt to see him in such a pathetic condition. If nothing else, at least now he was having these anxiety attacks in a safe environment. We kept our distance during those episodes and waited until Lance had repositioned himself away from the wall, a sign he had also gotten to a better place mentally.

One day, while reading in the living room, I happened to glance over at Lance. I thought he was sleeping, but something looked odd. He was lying on the floor, rigid and motionless, his eyes open but in a frozen stare. I called his name several times. No response. I feared he might be dead, but didn't have the nerve to touch him. *My own dog and I'm afraid to check for vital signs. If he's dead, should I bury him in the yard before Clara gets home so she won't have to see him or should I call her first? Do I even have the stomach to make such a call?* Then, he came to. It was like witnessing a resurrection. Later that day, I told Clara what had happened to prepare her should it happen in the future. It did. We were in the kitchen when Lance began walking toward us from the living room. His eyes lost that intense, I'm-running-this-show alertness and glazed over into a dead blankness, telegraphing trouble. As if in a trance, his body froze, this time while he was standing. He remained motionless, like a statue, for brief moments. We knew not to touch him. During such episodes, I'm not certain that he could see or hear us. We felt Lance was visiting another world and we'd have to wait for him to come back to ours. Fortunately, he was always able to make the return trip.

Other times, we noticed that a very faint quivering at one or both sides of his mouth, almost grin-like, meant he was in a bad place and we should stay away. He looked possessed. Sad to say, he probably was.

The most fear-provoking Lance? That was the dog that, while sitting or standing, emitted a steady stream of guttural growls that warned an all-out attack might soon follow. None ever did, maybe because Lance didn't have it in him, or maybe because we kept our distance until he came back to his senses.

One of Dr. Chambers' associates told me, "All dogs eventually respond to love." Apparently, Lance didn't get the memo. We gave him all the TLC we dared to, hoping he would respond appropriately. If insanity is doing the same thing over and over and expecting different results, than Clara and I were certifiable.

I formed my own admittedly unprofessional opinion as to Lance's dilemma. I remembered something called the approach/avoidance conflict from my college psychology courses. It refers to having a goal that is both desirable and undesirable. Lance still had a normal dog's wish to receive approving affection from his owner. Unfortunately, he also had a well-developed fear of being touched. So many times Lance approached one of us to be petted and then came unhinged: flinching, growling, snapping, or running away. The life he'd led had trapped him in an emotional bind from which he couldn't escape.

As he spent more time with us, it became evident that our dog's surly behavior was more out of defensiveness than viciousness. For one thing, he rarely followed up an initial attack with a second. For another, after acting out, Lance immediately banished himself to another room where he stayed—sometimes for several hours—apparently to sort things out. Following this self-imposed exile, he'd reappear, keeping a distance from us and wearing a look of regret as if saying, *Oh, look at what I've done!* Lying down close to one of us was Lance's signal that his time-out had ended. All would be well again, until the next time.

The whole thing was one big complicated and thankless task, like trying to make sense out of the senseless. What I'm sure seemed senseless to many was our ongoing attempt to form a bond with a dog that continually threatened us. I offer no explanation for the effort made other than our undying optimism.

-24-

Lance-isms

When not driving us to the point of despair, Lance entertained us with the lighter side of his personality.

Talk about quick conditioning! It's said that a Border Collie pays close attention to the slightest of details and Lance made me a believer. After watching me change to sneakers prior to our first few walks, Lance decided that whenever I donned that kind of footwear, we were headed on an excursion. To avoid his jumping to conclusions, I began putting on my gym shoes out of my dog's view. However, even when I sneakered-up in another room, once Lance saw me, he'd check out my feet. That quickly led to a look of intensive, inquisitive curiosity directed my way: *Are you trying to slip one past me?* In order to avoid his scrutiny, I got into the habit—or rather Lance got me into the habit—of going barefoot or in my stocking feet until it was time for me to leave, with or without him. Thanks to Lance, I spent the majority of my time in the house shoeless.

There were plenty of times Lance could care less what kind of footwear was or wasn't on my feet. If he'd made up his mind he wanted a walk that was that. He'd get an alert look on his face, activate those riveting eyes, and challenge me to a staring contest. If I looked away and then back at him, that stare was still there waiting for me. If I loitered, he'd leap to his feet and begin circling me. This was his way of letting me know he wanted one of his "scheduled" walks and I should share in his enthusiasm. Trying to ignore him was useless. He'd begin barking at the top of his lungs, browbeating me until he got his way.

In self-defense, I developed what proved to be a mediocre stalling tactic. Holding up my right hand, fingers spread open, I'd say "Five more minutes!" This would subdue Lance temporarily. Unfortunately, after a few minutes (five?) passed, the ritualistic circling would begin again. He might even bring me a sneaker to make his point. Lance's extra hearty barking made it clear he would not stand for any additional delay. I'd relent and off we'd go, my strategy buying me precious little time. My dog constantly herded me right out of my own house.

Although Jan Bittner said that staring at Lance might disturb or agitate him, *he* was the one who started all the staring contests. His purpose was always to badger me into taking him for another hike. His success rate was impressive.

More quick conditioning. One day while petting Lance I let out a hearty sneeze. From then on, whenever I sneezed he would rush over to me, expecting to be petted. Often I'd do all I could to camouflage a sneeze to avoid the dangers of touching my dog. It was difficult to sneak anything past Lance. Even a halfhearted or stifled *ahchoo* didn't go undetected. He'd sit there, head tilted, analyzing whatever kind of muffled sound I made, trying to determine if it rose to the level of a sneeze. Lance was the ultimate arbiter (there's a joke hidden in that word somewhere). All I could do was sit there and await his decision. If he decided I had attempted to pull a fast one on him, within seconds he'd be pestering me to pet him. It got to the point that during a sneezing fit I'd have the pleasure of multiple visits from the devil dog.

My dog and I often walked on a trail that passed by a horse corral. During our first visit, Lance greeted the equines with hearty, nonstop howling, which they ignored. In very short order, he accustomed himself to the four-legged steeds, no longer feeling the need to bark at them. In fact, on our many return visits there, not only did he roam with them in the pasture, he even came to take delight in feasting on fresh horse droppings. It was all I could do to keep Lance away from them (the droppings, not the horses).

Lance had excellent dining etiquette. When we were eating in the kitchen, he never entered to beg for food. He'd watch from the living room and patiently wait for any leftovers to be put down by his dish. Lance also never got into garbage cans or bags, not once. Perhaps because he had grown up living outside, he'd never developed some of the customs typical of a household canine.

Having been stuck outside for more than ten years, Lance greeted the alien sounds of a vacuum cleaner and coffeepot with continual barking during the first months of his domesticity. Eventually, he ignored them.

One sad note: Lance had a visible fear of any long-handled implement —broom, rake, mop, weed whacker, golf club, etc.—which he never got over. Whenever he spotted me holding any such item inside the house, he'd retreat to another room; if we were outside, he'd immediately take off for the farthest end of the yard and stay there until I had put the "weapon" completely out of sight.

–25–

Ambushed!

One day, after what had seemed an uneventful excursion through the woods, Lance and I returned home. Once inside, I picked up on a peculiarly foul odor. Pee-yu! It smelled like a dead animal, yet not exactly. In an effort to locate the source of this stench, I searched throughout the house, my dog following me. It was present in every room we entered. What in the world was going on?

Clara, done tending to her garden, came inside. She must be a bit more country than I, because she immediately said, "I bet Lance got skunked." I bent down next to Lance and did a smell test—of course, a quick one for my own safety. Sure enough, he was R-I-P-E!

Lance had not had a single bath during the first ten years of his existence. After rescuing him, our few attempts to bathe him were all unsuccessful; Lance's snapping and growling had seen to that. In spite of zero baths, Lance had always been a relatively odor-free dog. Now we faced a must-bathe situation, but no doubt Lance didn't think so. He always made it clear he would not stand for any kind of soaping, rinsing or drying.

Subjecting a dog groomer to the devil dog was out of the question, but I did put a call into a local pet boutique for advice. The groomer rattled off a combination of potential cleaning agents: hydrogen peroxide, baking soda, Dawn™ detergent, and a carbonated beverage. She said it might be up to several weeks before the smell was completely gone. I had to laugh when she stressed the importance of thoroughly drying off my dog. *Yeah, right!*

Then it hit me. On walks, Lance naturally gravitated to water: streams, lakes, ponds, etc. Presented with the opportunity, he'd eagerly wade in and then stand in place. This activity must have had a soothing effect on him, perhaps as much mentally as physically. With that in mind, I hooked Lance up to his leash. For him, this was the unmistakable sign we were going for yet another walk, so he was cooperative. He should have been suspicious of the fact his exhausted dad was volunteering for an additional march, so soon after the last one. He wasn't and out the door we went.

After leading him to the nearby Brodhead Creek, true to form he happily walked in. Following behind him, I readied a bottle of shampoo hidden in my shorts pocket. Lance assumed a relaxed stance. While nervously petting him with one hand I used my other to wet his coat with water from the stream. Then, I whipped out the shampoo bottle from my shorts pocket and began lathering him.

For a while Lance stared straight ahead, seemingly content and apparently oblivious to what was happening behind him. Then, he looked back at me quizzically, trying to figure out if he liked what was going on. Deciding he didn't, he snarled and flashed his teeth at me. That was his way of saying the bath was over. I got the message. Drying Lance by hand with a towel? That's another message I'd long ago gotten—don't bother trying! I walked a soaking wet dog home and let him spend the rest of the day drying out on his own.

Fortunately, in spite of the brevity of the bath and the fact I had used nothing more potent than my own shampoo, Lance smelled much better. In fact, within a few days, he was again his relatively non-pungent self. My dog could be called a lot of things, but definitely not a stinker.

Lance was twelve years old when he had his first bath. It was also his last. Somehow, except for that day, he managed to keep himself clean. It's a good thing because a truly thorough shampooing would have required muzzling and sedation, not usually offered at your local pet boutique.

-26-

Dissing the Don

As previously mentioned, within walking distance of our home sits a huge field complete with horse corral. Lance and I often strolled down Oak Tree Drive and onto this large open space. Once far enough removed from the road, I'd unleash my dog and he'd begin frolicking in every direction. Sometimes we'd cross the entire field and enter the deep woods behind it. This would lead to one of our mega-mile walks. Other times, I'd simply sit somewhere and let my dog run himself ragged (that would be the day!) in the field, roaming among the grazing horses, sniffing this and that, and occasionally breaking into wind sprints.

One afternoon we were on this field, I on the east side resting on a large rock, Lance some fifty yards to the west of me, busying himself among some bushes. I started savoring the fact that this was going to be one of those rare times that Lance did most all the walking. Life is good. It's a beautiful day, I'm relaxed, and Lance is behaving himself.

The growling began. I rushed across the field towards Lance, who was hidden behind some foliage. *What kind of beast has he stumbled onto this time?* As I got closer, I spotted him, along with a creature of the human variety he had flushed out from the bushes. It was Vinny, one of our neighbors, and not such a nice one. Vinny was a tall, heavyset, fifty-something mafia wannabee with a Joey Buttafuoco chin. He made it known throughout the neighborhood that he was in the mob (what mob I'm not sure—why, he doesn't even look like Al Pacino or sound like Marlon Brando).

Lance was circling him in a menacing fashion. Just as he began to lunge at Vinny, I corralled and leashed my dog. He kept trying to get at Vinny, so the ensuing conversation was short, but not particularly sweet.

Vinny muttered, "I always carry a gun. If that dog is ever on my property, I'll blow him away... and don't even think about calling the cops." I apologized profusely and told Vinny I hadn't seen him behind the bushes and certainly wouldn't have let my dog loose if I had. I also really didn't know what was eating Lance. I really didn't. When off our property, my dog tended to be standoffish around people, unless he was in herding mode. Possibly Lance had attempted to direct Vinny's movements and, when he didn't comply, my dog took issue.

That open field was scratched off our itinerary for the time being.

I'm still curious. Just what had Vinny been doing behind those bushes?

–27–

Border Collies will be Border Collies

Until meeting Lance the word collie had always conjured up images of Lassie, not a hyperactive black-and-white ball of fire like Lance. After taking Lance in, I read several books to familiarize myself with his breed. Although he had for so long lived a dysfunctional life, our dog still exhibited many of the traits that are typical of the Border Collie. To a degree, his essential nature had survived his abysmal lack of nurture.

Border Collies are known for their dynamism and need for exercise. In Canadensis, our house was surrounded by huge tracts of undeveloped land. Lance and I were free to take monumental hikes. Clara was never comfortable with my letting our dog loose anywhere. I admit I have a childish streak in me. I grew up in a thinly populated and thickly wooded area of Long Island. Yes, it's true. At one time, Long Island was not totally asphalted. Virtually everyone let their dogs run loose. As a youngster, I went outside a lot, as often as possible with my dog as a companion. Now I was trying to relive my youth through Lance, and this indefatigable dog was more than willing to help me do it. Lance and I took well over five thousand walks, many, thanks to my canine dynamo, lasting for hours.

A comical example of a Border Collie's dynamism: an acquaintance had a Border Collie that, unannounced, every so often tried to jump over her while she was sitting in her recliner. Sometimes he cleared her, sometimes he didn't.

The Border Collie also has a strong sense of direction. Only twice did Lance and I get separated while on a walk. In those instances, I was the one who got lost, and after finally finding my way home, there was Lance sitting on the porch steps with a look that begged the question *What took you so long?* My reply? "You're the herding dog, so why didn't you guide me home?" Naturally, he was left at a loss for words.

Border Collies are born with a shepherding instinct. Before moving to Canadensis, during one of our earliest sojourns on one of the Mount Minsi trails, we came up behind a group of some dozen or so hikers who were walking in single file immediately ahead of us. Without any prompting, Lance went into herding mode. Leaving me, he angled past the walkers up to the front and then, after leading us all for a while, he wound his way back to the end of the line to make sure there were no stragglers. His work didn't stop until we all reached the parking lot. To my great relief, he did all this without biting anyone. I was uneasy during the entire process. Although he hadn't yet threatened anyone when with me, I just wasn't sure about his trustworthiness around people. Little had I known what was to come.

That incident was no fluke. There was another day when I was walking with my two preteen granddaughters, Krystyl and Aryanna, in the woods near my Mount Bethel apartment. Krystyl had wandered off the beaten path and gotten herself entangled in the brush. Without any prompting on my part, Lance went about the business of directing her out of the brambles and back onto the path, where Aryanna and I were waiting.

Once in Canadensis, this instinct also manifested itself inside the house. Lance, like any self-respecting herding dog, much preferred that we remain in his line of vision, appearing most relaxed when all three of us were in the same room. If such was not the case, unlike some others of his breed, he rarely felt compelled to conduct a roundup and then contain us in one room with him. Lance graciously extended some liberties to us, his flock. He'd put himself at ease by patrolling from room to room, verifying our continued existence.

Fortunately for us, Lance never took this herding tendency to the extreme some of his counterparts do. A few years prior to meeting Lance, I did volunteer work at a local pet rescue operation. A Border Collie by the name of Scooter had been given up by a family tired of always being crammed together in the same room at Scooter's insistence.

This leads to another Border Collie feature, those piercing eyes. The *I-will-not-be-ignored!* eyes. In fact, no words completely describe them. One has to see them, and be seen by them, to fully appreciate their intensity. Undoubtedly, they greatly assist with watching and controlling a herd of animals. As Lance grew older and, at times, seemingly mellower, his stare occasionally would take on a look of pure adoration of his owners. In those situations, if I'd acknowledge him, Lance would come over to be petted. Lucky me!

SCENE OF THE TEN YEAR CRIME, MINUS THE DOGHOUSE

WELCOME TO MY NIGHTMARE

FROM THE DOGHOUSE TO THE PENTHOUSE

MY BEST CHRISTMAS EVER!

LANCE CRAMMING HIMSELF INTO THE CAT'S BED

TAKING A FIVE MINUTE BREAK BETWEEN FIVE-MILE HIKES

STAY AWAY! WE DID.

DON'T HURT ME! WE DIDN'T.

AUTHOR NERVOUSLY ACTING "AS IF"

-28-

Hell on Wheels

THE GREAT PLEASURE OF A DOG IS THAT YOU MAY MAKE A
FOOL OF YOURSELF WITH HIM AND NOT ONLY WILL HE NOT
SCOLD YOU, BUT HE WILL MAKE A FOOL OF HIMSELF TOO.

– SAMUEL BUTLER, BRITISH AUTHOR

One warm sunny early-spring afternoon, I volunteered myself for hazardous duty—taking Lance back to Mount Minsi just for old time's sake. The hazardous part? The car ride.

Clara dis-invited herself. She refused to relax her policy of not getting into any motor vehicle featuring the devil dog as a passenger. She wanted no part of his in-car antics. Clara was sensible that way; I wasn't. The guy who said that a fool doesn't get to live long never met me.

First, a safety check: seat belt on, all doors locked, and windows rolled all the way up. With my dog sitting quietly next to me in the front seat, I started the car and let it idle longer than was my custom. It wasn't so much to let the car warm up, but rather about allowing myself some peace and quiet before the inevitable storm broke out.

Lance didn't disappoint. The minute we began backing out of the driveway, he sprang into action. Yes, this would be a ride like every other with this dog. A sensible person would have ended the drive immediately. That's why I didn't.

On our way to Mount Minsi everything was par for the course—I drove while Lance jumped and flailed his way around the car's interior. As the chaos continued, I had to chuckle to myself. I'd read in a book that "if you accustom your Border Collie to car rides early, he will always be eager to jump in and go along." Well, Lance didn't get accustomed until late in his life, but he still was always eager to jump in and go along. The trouble was, once the car started moving, he'd keep on jumping.

Lance had convinced me long ago it was pointless to set up any restraints for him in the car. He was stronger than anything I could come up with. Why couldn't he just settle down and act like a normal dog? I kept hoping that each "next time" he got into the car would be the one during which he finally acclimated himself to being a passenger. This time was obviously not going to be that "next time." Message to self: *No more lengthy rides with Lance.*

At least I could predict each impending outburst and brace myself. Once a vehicle in the oncoming lane neared mine, eagle-eyes sprang into action. He barked and lunged at the enemy car as it approached, while it was passing, and for a short while after it had gone by. Then he'd alertly sit until the next vehicle caught his attention. Every single car was fair game. According to the experts, a dog in a moving vehicle barking at objects passing by is exhibiting predatory behavior. It was at least comforting to know that Lance was after what lay outside my car, not the driver sitting inside it.

I prayed for light traffic. Why? To avoid the bedlam that resulted from heavy traffic. If a string of cars passed by, Lance issued a matching string of ear-piercing barks, one for each vehicle as it passed. Sometimes, when it looked like a vehicle had slipped through his radar, Lance would rush to the back and, from the rear hatch window, content himself with barking at the car's taillights. *Thought I missed you, eh?*

For whatever reason, Lance never showed interest in any car I followed in my lane. A car behind me was a different story. If no cars were passing us and there was one in back of us, Lance would fly to the backseat, look out the rear window, and bark his brains out. His noisemaking went on for as long as the vehicle kept following me. I often found myself praying, in the name of peace and quiet, that it would turn off and head somewhere else. On the other hand, Lance occupied in the back seat was less meddlesome than in the front seat. Pick your poison.

In spite of his best efforts, every once in a while a car would sneak past Lance's scrutiny. I silently celebrated.

Then there were all the people to concern himself with—so many pedestrians, so little time. There also were those inanimate objects. He couldn't let them off the hook, could he? Each time we passed a mailbox, parking meter, fire hydrant, traffic sign, or anything else that caught his eye, Lance went berserk.

Lance seemed especially energetic today. Maybe he had spring fever. I spent a good deal of the drive with one hand on the wheel and the other staving off Lance's attempted assaults at certain passing targets, specifically the ones that had him jumping on my lap and barking out my window. Occasionally, I had to use both hands in my attempts to control him. Thanks (if that's the right word) to Lance, I was mastering the art of managing the steering wheel with my knees so I could fend off the devil dog with both hands. Unfortunately, I hadn't quite perfected the technique.

Lance was keeping himself, and me, so busy I missed the turnoff for the park and had to drive several miles past it before I could swing around and backtrack. That meant spending additional unwanted time with Lance in a moving vehicle. For that, I would pay dearly.

On a particularly twisting turn along northbound Route 611, Lance's interference caused us to swerve sharply to the right onto a way-too-narrow shoulder. Several cars were right behind me, so I couldn't get back on the road without getting slammed. For a split second, I saw only two options: stay on the shoulder and risk side-swiping a metal railing or cut the wheel sharply to the right, drive through an opening in the railing, and take a ride down a seventy-foot hill. Surviving that, we'd be able to continue our drive—in the Delaware River. Fortunately, I wouldn't have to do either. The railing mercifully ended, and I was able to bring my car to a screeching stop on a wider portion of the shoulder. After collecting my wits, I eased back onto Route 611.

It was time to vent.

"Lance (I only used his given name when I was at my wits' end with him; doing that signaled that I meant business.), one way or another you're going to be the death of me." The truth was we both had a reckless streak, so more likely we were going to be the death of each other.

I pulled my car back onto the road, still collecting my thoughts after that near miss. Just moments later, I was again grabbing Lance with both hands while maneuvering my car with my left knee (it can be done, but not well), causing us to briefly cross over the double yellow line into the oncoming lane. Unfortunately, there happened to be a car in that oncoming lane. Looking up from our wrestling match, I saw the vehicle headed right at us. I threw Lance away from me, grabbed the wheel with both hands, and swerved back into my lane. In my side view mirror I saw the other car fishtailing in a cloud of dust before coming to a stop on the shoulder. We had been this close to a head-on collision. I felt the rush of adrenaline and the prickly skin that come with a close shave. Lance, on the other hand, appeared quite unmoved by the whole thing.

Before I could fully savor the joy of still being alive, I heard a siren and saw a police car in my rearview mirror. My first reaction was to get mad at Lance. "Ya damn mutt! You're going to cost me money and points on my license. You're really the one that wanted to come to Mount Minsi (conveniently forgetting it was my idea). If it wasn't for you, I wouldn't be in this position." He ignored me. I looked directly at him. "You are without a doubt the world's worst car passenger." Lance didn't have anything to say. How could he? His behavior was indefensible and he knew it—I think.

Funny how life's priorities can change so quickly. Seconds ago, I was grateful just to still be alive. Now all I could think about was how much this little adventure was going to cost me financially.

Unfortunately knowing the drill a bit too well (I have a heavy foot), I pulled my car into a parking area that featured a scenic view and sat glumly. I, for one, had no interest in taking in the sights. I watched the patrol car—State Police, to top it off—pull up behind me and come to a stop. A trooper got out and started heading my way. When he reached my car, I made the mistake of opening my window too much.

"Sir, your license and…"

Lance had been sitting calmly (naturally, the car was stopped) next to me in the front passenger seat. Upon seeing the officer, he lunged in the air towards my open window and was about to exit the car on the fly. His destination? A Pennsylvania State Trooper. I grabbed him around the neck with my right hand to stop his flight, while my left hand feverishly rolled up the window, leaving it open just a crack. Lance (now sitting on my lap), the trooper, and I proceeded to have a three-way conversation. Lance's contribution was a combination of barks, growls, and whines.

Over Lance's noise pollution the trooper yelled, "Sir please get your license, registration and proof of insurance, and get out of the car. I want your keys. (Eyeing Lance warily) Keep that dog in the car."

He didn't realize how difficult a task that was. Lance had never met the door that could stop him.

Already a basket case from the near accident, now I was looking at tickets and fines, all of this courtesy of Lance. Yeah, I know. I was still blaming the dog.

With Lance on my lap, I collected the requested paperwork and prepared myself for a grand exit. Fortunately, I had brought along dog treats. Taking out a chicken strip from my pocket, I threw it into the far corner of the rear seat. Lance went for the bait. That gave me the few seconds I needed to jump out of the driver's door and slam it behind me.

Seconds later, Lance, probably feeling he had just been duped by the old "chicken strip trick," pressed himself against the driver's window, pawing and clawing like the maniac he was.

The trooper began talking to me in that official-sounding, humorless, law enforcement monotone, while a few feet away a rabid animal was trying to break through a window to get at him. I suggested we move further from the car in the name of peace and quiet. Trooper Bevins (per his nameplate) agreed.

He went back to his car to run a check on me, leaving me standing in the parking lot.

With the trooper busy, I walked over to my car and got back to the business of scolding Lance. Just because I didn't have any common sense was no excuse for him to have none. He was perched on the front passenger seat. I talked to him through the slightly opened driver's window.

"Other people have normal dogs they can ride with. Not me. I got stuck with you. You know, you could be replaced by a real dog."

Lance turned his back to me and began looking out the passenger window. Perhaps something had caught his attention, or maybe I had hurt his feelings.

Guilt set in. "I'm sorry, Boobeeka. I'm the parent. I should have known better than taking this drive. I know it's probably pointless to say this, but please just try to behave for the next few minutes. Let's not make things worse."

I had the distinct feeling Lance was tuning me out. I was saved from further fruitless reasoning with him when Trooper Bevins returned from his vehicle. Being a drug and alcohol counselor, I immediately recognized the apparatus in his hand.

Scrutinizing my eyes carefully he asked me, "Mr. Stoffel, have you had anything to drink today?"

"No sir."

"Would you object to a breathalyzer?"

"No."

He administered the test. I passed the audition. Our conversation continued.

"Mr. Stoffel, are you on any type of medication?"

"No."

"So sir, how would you explain the stunt driving I just witnessed?"

"I have a very hyperactive dog. I usually can control him better."

"Why in the world would you have a dog like that loose in your car?"

"Sir—"

He quickly corrected me. "Trooper Bevins."

"Trooper Bevins, to be honest, I've tried lots of ways to restrain him, ropes, even put up barricades. Nothing works. I usually can control him with my hands."

"(Reeking with skepticism) So let me get this straight. You can't stop him with ropes or anything, but you usually control him by hand? Who's driving while you are doing this? He's a menace. I'm thinking I should impound your car... I don't know. It'd be the first time I had to impound a car because of a dog."

The two of us stood there awhile in an uncomfortable silence, at least uncomfortable for me. I guessed the trooper was deciding what legal charges to hit me with.

"Do you usually leash your dog?"

"Yes," I lied.

"You have one in the car?"

"Yes." *(Whew! Thank God I brought it!)*

"Look, I want you to leash him—short leash, very short—and..."

Trooper Bevins circled my car, examining the interior. From inside, Lance greeted him at each window with a toothy snarl.

"There's a ring behind the back seat, for a cargo net. Run the leash clip end through it and hook him up. That'll hold him. The leash handle is way bigger than the ring. He won't go anywhere. Hook him up. I don't care where you were going, take him back home now. Oak Tree Drive, right?"

"Yes sir, er...Trooper. That's right."

"I'm going to be following you. If there are any problems, I'm going to have to impound the car, and if I do that, I'll be giving you some summonses. You have a commercial license. I'm trying to give you a break."

"Understood. Thanks for your tolerance, sir... uh...Trooper Bevins." Was I groveling? You bet I was.

After he returned my keys to me, I asked the officer to move away from my car so that Lance would calm down, making my reentry easier and my dog less likely to spring loose. The fact that Lance went after civilians was bad enough. If he bit an officer of the law, no doubt there'd be absolute hell to pay.

Opening the door ever so slightly, I sucked in my stomach and squeezed myself into the car while pushing Lance over onto the front passenger seat.

Clambering into the back seat, I reached behind it and pushed the clip of the leash though the ring. Curious, Lance climbed over the front seat rest and sat next to me, unaware his days of rollicking in the car were ending right before his very eyes. I fastened the leash clip onto Lance's collar. The leash handle was way too big; there was no possibility it could slip through the ring holding it. With this set-up, Lance had to sit firmly planted in the rear seat. Lance stuck in the back seat—I was really beginning to like this idea.

After getting into the driver's seat, I gave Trooper Bevins a thumbs-up. If a stupid leash didn't hold up, I would be walking home car-less and with a pocketful of summonses—and my passenger could care less. Ridiculous. But, I had only myself to blame for being in this situation.

There was no point in ordering Lance to stay calm until the policeman stopped tailing us. He'd tune me out. I could only hope that the leashing arrangement would hold up at least long enough to get the trooper off my back.

We were ready to roll, I in the front, Lance secured in the back. He was quiet and calm until the car started moving. Then, as if on cue, Lance began barking and pulling on the leash.

He couldn't break loose; he was contained. *Hey, this is a pretty good setup. I should've thought of it long ago. Wait until I tell Clara we can start planning some real vacations utilizing the car.* (In my euphoria I didn't bother to consider the complications of traveling with a four-legged beast that, no matter where we went, upon arrival would have to be quarantined from the rest of civilization. A vacation with Lance would have been no vacation.) Even his barking was like music to my ears, since it wasn't accompanied by a completely out-of-control dog bouncing around in the car and making the ride a total nightmare.

We proceeded along Route 611, Lance straining to get free, barking all the while. It was comical watching him try to threaten passing cars while straightjacketed.

Through the Delaware Water Gap and onto Route 80 West the trio went: I kept driving, Lance kept struggling, and the officer kept following.

The first exit off Route 80 was mine. I turned on my directional and headed onto the ramp.

Something was happening in the back seat. I got the feeling my dog's efforts to escape were beginning to pay off, at least for him. A look in my rearview mirror confirmed my suspicions. Lance had increased his wiggle room. I'd seen him get out of all kinds of setups we'd rigged in the car. Whatever had made me think this one would work?

While driving on the curved part of the exit ramp, I glanced in the rearview mirror. There was no police car in sight, but I couldn't fully relax until getting back on the straightaway, from which I'd get a fuller view of traffic behind me.

Lance was now able to touch the back of my seat with his paws. He kept lunging ahead, trying to break free.

Finally, I got onto Route 191. Looking in my rearview mirror, there was not a police car to be seen. What a relief! Since meeting Lance, this was the farthest we had ever driven without my suffering his intrusiveness. It was a pleasure, a pleasure that wouldn't last much longer.

Snap! The leash was still attached to his collar, but it was no longer restraining him. Lance was free to do what he did best—go insane. Ah, the best laid plans of mice and State Troopers.

I checked all my mirrors. Thankfully, not one official-looking vehicle in sight. We had about seven miles to go. Lance, free to roam, made them seven very interesting miles. Interesting, as in horrendous.

After arriving home I inspected my dog's handiwork. Lance, with herculean strength, had broken the leash's restraining mechanism—an extra heavy duty leash, no less. It was permanently stuck at its maximum length. Not so surprising, once I reminded myself that he had snapped his run on numerous occasions while on the Schmidt property. Once again, the irresistible force had overcome an immovable object.

We didn't make it to Mount Minsi and wouldn't be trying again anytime soon. My recklessness had almost gotten both of us killed, along with people in another car or two. Why was I still acting like a teenager? Maybe today had taught me the lesson I so badly needed to learn.

In the interest of domestic tranquility, this was one of those escapades Clara didn't need to know about. I was confident Lance would keep our secret.

-29-

Damning Evidence

The first day of every week I teach GED courses at two correctional facilities in New Jersey. My drive home from that work takes me through Portland, Pennsylvania, a town lying right next to Mount Bethel. There's an ice cream stand in Portland called Kelly's—the best ice cream stand I have ever gone to, bar none. It's open from May through Labor Day and each Monday, during the summer, I have to force myself to not stop there. One particular Monday, my sugar cravings got the best of me. I pulled into Kelly's and, after ordering a vanilla thick shake float with extra malt, sat down on one of the benches there. Before even finishing it, the thought of getting a refill had already popped into my head. As I mentally battled with my sweet tooth, a fortyish auburn-haired woman and a teenaged girl approached me, each with an ice cream cone.

"Are you the man that used to walk that black-and-white dog, you know, Lance, the Schmidts' dog?"

"Yes."

"I'm almost afraid to ask. What ever happened to him?"

"I have him."

"Really? You do? Thank God. Unbelievable. When a dog disappears from that property, you always kind of assume the worst."

"They've had others?"

"There was the one that supposedly got hit by a car. (Sarcastically) Yeah right, probably by *their* car. That one and the one they had before Lance."

"They had a dog before Lance?"

"Not for long. They kept him chained outside next to the garage. He looked like a Shepherd, knowing them, probably a purebred. I've heard they like to brag about how expensive their dogs are. He didn't last more than a few months and then one day—gone. I guess it was a little while later they got the black-and-white (Lance)."

"Yeah, the Schmidts are quite a crew."

"By the way, my name's Rachel; this is my daughter Jenny."

Without prompting, Rachel sat down with her daughter and began a soliloquy, almost a confessional.

"You know, talking to you is reminding me of something I'd just as soon forget. I'll probably never be able to forget it anyway. Everybody had to know they abused the dog; I actually got to see it. I was driving past the Schmidt property and caught Ted, you know, their son, in the act. The dog was trying to get to his feet and Ted was standing over him with a shovel in his hand. It was pretty obvious that he'd just whacked the dog with it. I hit the horn and Ted turned and looked at me. I didn't really know what else to do so I wagged my finger at him. He put down the shovel. The dog kind of staggered into his doghouse. Ted started walking back to the house. I drove away, but something was bugging me so, I don't know why, something told me to circle around the block. What I saw made me sick. You know, I'm more of a cat person but geez, how do you do that to any animal? My god. Now that idiot was stooped down in front of the doghouse poking the shovel into it, you know, jabbing at the dog. The guy is an SOB all around. Did you know he used to beat up his mother? Maybe he still does. Anyway, so I roll down the window and tell him, 'I'm calling the cops.' He says to me, 'Go ahead you fuc... (glancing at Jenny) bitch.' He stood up and dropped the shovel and started giving me the finger with both hands. I didn't have my cell phone, but I pretended I did and made like I was dialing. He must've figured I was 'cause he started going towards the house. But this time I waited until he went inside. I did another slow loop around the block and passed again. Ted wasn't in sight. I was relieved because I could picture him coming after *me* with the shovel. That's how crazy they are. I figured Lance was in his doghouse. I couldn't see him from the road. I'd have checked on him but, to tell you the truth, I was always afraid of him and I was really afraid of his owners. No way I'm going on their property. They are completely nuts. I'm surprised I had the guts to even threaten to call the cops."

I responded. "Well, based on what I know about 'em, the Schmidts definitely aren't my idea of a good time."

Rachel continued. "When I got home, I called 911. That wasn't the right number to call but I was too nervous to think straight. They referred me to animal control, the ASPCA, something like that. I got a machine and left a message. (Laughing) Just my phone number, no name. That's how scared of the Schmidts I am. I never got a call back. Later on, I think

I called the police. They sent me back to animal control. A report was taken. You know how that goes."

"So the eventual outcome was…"

"Nothing. I never heard anything from anybody. I finally got involved and nothing happened. Like I said, just about everybody knew what was going on there, but nothing happened about it. I don't know what else I could've done. To be honest, after that I avoided going by that house again for a *long* time. The whole thing made me feel sick and kind of guilty. Personally, I think that woman who walks all their dogs is nuts too. She's got to know what they do to their dogs."

"But, of course I walked him too. I took over for Anna."

"I'm sorry. I didn't mean…"

"That's okay. Every once in a while back then I questioned what I was doing myself."

"So anyway, one day a long time after, I drive by and everything is gone, the doghouse, everything. All I could think was R.I.P. That is one dog-unfriendly property. I don't know how that dog made it all that time."

"Well, one of my many nicknames for Lance is Die-hard."

"You got that right."

Jenny asked, "Mom, what about Sean and Richie?"

"Geez, what a pair. Jenny's cousins. Real losers. They've got to be somewhere in their late twenties by now. Jenny found out they used to throw rocks at the poor dog."

"Even when he was in his doghouse," her daughter added. "They'd throw them inside it."

"One day Jack caught them. He made them pick up every single stone on his lawn. I'm sure he didn't give a rat's ass about his dog—it was his precious lawn. So you have Lance. I can't believe it. Amazing. Let me ask you something. Does he ever come after you?"

"Sometimes."

"I knew it! Wow. You know, one time I saw him wandering around here in Portland. He was dragging whatever that wire thing was they kept him tied up with. Even though he was walking right around here on 611 (a busy thoroughfare), I have to admit I didn't do anything. I wouldn't have dared to let him into my car. Angela—she lives near me—saw him loose walking around on her property once too. People tended to keep their distance from him. He scared people. Can't say as I blame him, but how do you deal with it?"

"I'm not exactly sure. Sometimes I wonder myself. I didn't know he had a biting problem until it was too late—you know, we'd taken him. But I could never take him back to them (the Schmidts). Besides, he's been doing pretty well lately. My wife and I have our fingers crossed."

"Between me and you, did you steal him?"

"No."

"Hey, it's all right. You can tell me. I'd never tell those idiots."

"No, technically we had their permission, maybe not their blessing, but their permission."

"I'm very pleasantly surprised. Amazed really. When I saw the dog-house gone, I figured it was just another mysterious disappearance. I felt I should have done something more. I was guilty for so long."

"Hey, don't feel bad. I used to jog right past Lance for years. I didn't do anything."

"Yeah, but after that day I actually knew for sure how they treated him. I figured he'd died because I didn't follow up. You just put an end to my guilt trip. Then, like I said, the next one supposedly got hit by a car. It's so wrong that they keep getting dogs. The way I look at it there's nothing wrong with not liking dogs, but there's something very wrong about not liking dogs and continually having them. It just doesn't make any sense. Maybe they should have a Children and Youth agency for pets. Well...by the way I didn't get your name."

"Walter."

"Walter. Nice meeting you. Jenny's got soccer."

"Nice meeting both of you."

"I'll keep an eye on their latest dog. Maybe you could take him too."

"No thank you. One psycho dog is enough. Actually, like I said, I've been kind of optimistic that Lance could be finally turning the corner."

"Well, I hope he does, for your sake as well as his."

As if on cue, we all stood up. Rachel and her daughter headed for the parking area. I, on the other hand, went back to the stand for more ice cream. In addition to another malted for myself, I bought a cup of ice cream. Not for Clara. She was on a diet. It was for Lance. He wasn't a weight watcher. Besides, after what I had just listened to, it seemed like the right thing to do. Strawberry. Two scoops.

-30-

Protective Custody

"Get rid of that effin' mutt or he's dead meat. Got it?" (Click).

Clara hung up the phone. Her face was ashen.

"What was that all about?"

"Someone just threatened to kill Lance."

"What? Do you know who it was?"

"I didn't recognize the voice."

"Male or female?"

"Male."

"Did he say why?"

"No. He hung up right away."

I checked the caller I.D. "Caller unknown." I hit redial. The number was blocked. The only thing worse than a death threat is an anonymous death threat.

Clara looked at me suspiciously—almost accusingly.

"Have you gotten into any trouble with him lately?"

"No."

"Well, why would anyone make a call like that?"

"I wonder if Chuck is still pissed off about what happened to Diablo." Diablo was Chuck's dog that Lance had sent to the hospital—at my expense.

It had all started innocently enough. I noticed that, when we were outside, if I broke into a run, Lance tended to run alongside me. One day, I decided not to bother leashing Lance prior to his walk. My plan was for us to run across the street and immediately enter the woods. What could possibly go wrong? A lot.

On this particular day, Diablo, living directly across the street from us, happened to be outside and also unleashed. These two had never met, as we made every effort to keep Lance away from dogs as well as people. Diablo had been lying on his owner's driveway, but upon seeing Lance, sprang to his feet and rushed towards us on the street. I sprinted for the woods, hoping Lance would follow me. Instead he stood still, awaiting Diablo's arrival. I called for my dog to come to me, to no avail. Diablo began sniffing Lance. I became cautiously optimistic—without good reason, as it turned out. Lance returned Diablo's sniff down with a smackdown. He got into full-attack mode, making my commands worthless.

Although the two dogs were about the same size, the fight quickly became a mismatch with Lance inflicting all the damage. I watched in horror as a domestic pet struggled against a semi-feral beast.

If Lance had his way, this was going to be a fight to the death. I grabbed him by the collar. He whirled his head around and let out an unearthly growl. For a split second, I thought he was going to switch gears and come after me. Rather, he had only been distracted momentarily from the task at hand. He went back at Diablo, dragging me along with him. Do I keep trying to pull Lance away from Diablo and risk aggravating my dog to the point of getting bitten, or let go and… do what?

Lance sunk his teeth deeply into his opponent's abdomen. Diablo let out a yelp and hightailed it for his owner's porch. Thankfully, Lance must have felt he had made his point as he showed no interest in finishing off his victim. Donna, Chuck's wife, was at her front door and she immediately opened it to let her dog in. Diablo had met the real "devil dog."

After coaxing Lance back into our house, I went over to ask Donna how her dog was doing. He had a nasty open wound in his stomach that required medical attention.

"Why in the world do you keep that dog? He bites Clara for God's sake, and I saw him go after the termite man. You should get rid of him. If I ever see him off a leash again, I'm calling the cops. I'm telling you that right now."

Chuck called me that night. I didn't bother to point out that technically the fight had occurred on neutral territory and that his dog had also been unleashed. Instead, since Lance's reputation preceded him, I apologized profusely, offering to pay any medical costs. Two weeks later Donna showed up at my front door with a vet bill of $800.

That incident had occurred six or seven months before the threatening phone call. At first glance, six or seven months struck me as a long time to still be angry over a dog fight. Then I asked myself, *How would I feel if I continued to live across the street from a "wild" animal after it had attacked my normal dog? Wouldn't I feel just like Chuck probably did—on edge and angry?*

More recently, there had been another "interesting" episode. Nearby the horse farm Lance and I often visited sits a former motel converted to year-round rental apartments. These units rest on a hill overlooking the farm and back up to an area of the state forest we often walked in. One day, on my return from a hike in those woods, I approached the edge of the forest where it borders the horses' grazing pasture. Though not sure of my dog's exact whereabouts, I assumed he was somewhere in the general vicinity and would bolt out into the open any second. That's when I heard an angry "Get the hell offa my property!" quickly followed by Lance's unmistakable—and highly menacing—growls, mixed together with some of his most energetic barking. All of this came from the direction of the apartments so I rushed towards them. Arriving, I spotted Lance. He had wandered onto the common driveway that led from the rentals to the main road. Facing him stood a man, wobbly on his feet, a beer in one hand and a baseball bat in the other. He clumsily swung it at Lance, narrowly missing him. I yelled "Come!" to my dog. He ignored me, too wrapped up in his confrontation with the stranger. After screaming "Get the hell out of here, you fuckin' mutt," the man swung the bat again, this time losing his balance, and his beer, and hitting the ground. I had to get Lance out of there, but I didn't have the guts to grab him by the collar, not after seeing his reaction when I tried that during his skirmish with Diablo. Again I yelled "Come!", this time running back into the woods, hoping Lance would interpret my actions as a sign we were going on another hike. My plan worked and Lance charged after me. I continued deeper into the woods, putting as much distance as possible between us and Lance's assailant. From far off an unfriendly voice warned, "Keep that mutt off my property. Next time I'll shoot 'im.'"

We made our way home via a roundabout and—much to Lance's liking —lengthier route. On the way, I struggled to jar my memory. *Where had I seen that man's face before?* Then I remembered. Months earlier, a state trooper had visited our house, advising us that a Megan's Law parolee would be moving into the neighborhood. He showed us a photo of a balding, ruddy-faced sixty-something-year-old male. The photo had grabbed my attention because the face in it looked like every child's worst nightmare. He was even more gruesome in person. Being familiar with the legal system, I had no doubt he was violating his parole by drinking alcohol ("...I'll shoot 'im"? *Did he have firearms too?*). I had no interest in dropping the dime on him, but, from that day on, made sure Lance and I steered clear of those apartments. Would a parolee take the risk of making a threatening phone call and possibly go even further? Some would, and maybe this guy was one of them.

Of course, our neighbor Vinny couldn't be ruled out either. He'd had that run-in with Lance on a nearby field. A Cosa Nostra type—as Vinny imagined himself to be—is known for holding on to grudges and doing something about them. You just never know about people.

There was something else that I hadn't shared with Clara that I did now—a problem of my own that may have led to this threatening phone call. Recently, my hip had started giving me trouble. The orthopedist said I was losing cartilage. At times, the hip hurt like hell, but Lance didn't want to hear any excuses. He would not let his exercise schedule be modified. His relentless "hounding" forced me into taking what had become excruciatingly painful walks. When my discomfort was particularly severe, and if Clara wasn't at home, I'd let Lance out on his own. Sure it was unwise but—well, you know, anything after "but" is...

I had no idea where Lance was going on these solo excursions. He didn't stay outdoors for more than fifteen or twenty minutes before he'd come back home. Clearly he didn't find walking alone as exciting as traveling with his owner. Nevertheless, Lance on the loose could do a lot of damage in fifteen minutes. How many people had he threatened when outside alone? This admission elicited a lecture from Clara about my irresponsibility, which in turn elicited no rebuttal. A flawed dog had a flawed owner—me.

There was yet another incident that may have provoked a neighbor. I hadn't advised Clara about this event either, and didn't plan to since I was still licking my wounds from the above-mentioned scolding. One day several weeks earlier, while Clara was at work, I was home bringing firewood inside and stacking it near the fireplace. The side storm door was propped open to make my entry while carrying logs easier. Lance tagged along every time I left the house and then reentered with me. At some point, nature called. While I was in the bathroom, Lance began to bark from somewhere in the house. There followed brief quiet and then the barking resumed—outside the house. *The side door is open!* I rushed outdoors just in time to see Lance—well, at least a black tail with a white tip— disappear into the woods behind our house. I called out his name, but I knew obeying me would not likely be his main priority. I wondered what was.

After grabbing my jacket and a leash, I scrambled into the woods, hoping I'd spot my dog. Too late. Lance was nowhere to be seen or heard. Where to head in search of him? The trouble with dogs is, in the woods, they leave invisible paw-prints. If I had to guess, and that's all I could do, he'd given chase to a deer and could be anywhere by now. Behind our house lay vast acres of extremely dense woods, in which were a few dirt roads and even fewer houses. Looking for Lance in that maze would be like looking for the proverbial needle.

Having no plan of action, I sat down on a large rock and waited. I didn't know where Lance was, but maybe he'd find me. The still grayness of an overcast, chilly late fall afternoon provided a somber backdrop for my growing discomfort. Fiddling with the leash, I occasionally called out "Lance!" and got more concerned each time there was no response. Five, maybe ten minutes went by. Then, a soft tapping on my back startled me. Certain it wasn't Lance, who or what could it be? Another tap. I turned around. It was Winky, our cat. He was just saying hello. After petting him, he stretched out next to me on the rock. We both waited.

Bam! Bam! Bam! The report of a rifle. Then a dog's barking—surely Lance's. Bam! Bam! This time the only thing that followed was the rifle's echo. This second round was sufficient to send Winky heading for cover. I listened intently, hoping, praying to hear my dog's bark. Nothing. The stillness returned.

That's right—it's still hunting season! Panic set in. I could no longer just sit and wait. It was time to actively search for my dog, though not knowing where to begin and fearing what I might find.

I headed in the general direction from which the rifle shots had come, shouting a nonstop stream of now desperate sounding "Here Lance(s)." Not one of my calls got a response. Now after four o'clock, it was beginning to get dark so I upped my walking pace.

Although moving quickly as if with a purpose, I really had no idea where to begin looking. Some of these woods were turf Lance and I had traveled, some weren't. There were various houses, maybe five or ten, scattered about the area. These were a mixture of newer, more expensive homes owned by New York and New Jersey transplants and older, much more modest cabins, the properties of locals. I always steered clear of all of these residences because of Lance.

"Here Lance! Here boy!" My calls were now less frequent and less enthusiastic, because his lack of response was getting to me. I mentally kicked myself for not having closed the door at home. Had I sent my own dog to his death?

Bam! Bam! Bam! More blasts and much closer, again followed only by a rifle's echoes. The idealist in me couldn't believe someone would actually shoot a dog; the realist in me could. Most likely as a hunting accident, but there was another scenario to consider. After all, this was Lance, at times a very menacing dog. Most everyone else in the world wouldn't be as tolerant of him as Clara and I were. Had he threatened the wrong person?

From the woods, I spotted a dirt road and walked out onto it. With the sun almost set, I could see lights coming from a few houses off in the distance. Between the gunfire and the quickly darkening sky, I felt uncomfortable for my own well-being, as well as full of dread for Lance's.

Many times on our walks we'd get separated along the way and then reunite before heading home. Tough to picture something like that happening this time. There were even a couple of times we had gone our own ways and not met up again until getting back to the house, where Lance would be waiting for me on the stoop. I didn't see that happening today either.

The very strong possibility that someone may have shot Lance sickened me. What a horrible end to what had been for so long such a horrible life. I was determined to find out what had happened to my dog and get it over with. I could not go back home and just sit there, waiting for him to show up. There was nothing to feed my optimism that he would or even could make it back.

The road I was on led back to Route 447, close to its intersection with Oak Tree Drive. My plan was to head for my house, get a flashlight, and continue the search.

Bam! Bam! These shots came from deep in the woods south of me. There were a couple of houses in that general area. Maybe an already injured Lance had just been finished off, maybe he had dodged the earlier shots only to be hit with the latest round, or maybe—I desperately hoped— all the shooting had nothing to do with him.

The only light to guide me was coming from a now suddenly cloud-free sky full of bright stars and a three-quarter moon. I was on a dirt path just yards from a main road when a fast-moving *crunch, crunch* hit my ears. Something or someone was about to burst out of the woods just ahead of me. Then I heard it—the unmistakable sound of Lance's whining! He popped out onto the road and rushed up to me. I gave him a quick once-over. No blood. Thank God! I couldn't believe our luck. That whining was his reaction to the most recent volley of shots—oh, how he hated loud noises. I hooked him up and we headed home double-time.

What actually happened that autumn day? Had Lance threatened one of our neighbors living behind us? Or had he simply wandered onto somebody's yard and been greeted with gunfire? Or had he not been a target at all? As of that day, the woods behind our house became officially off-limits for all future walks.

The threatening phone call served as a wake-up call. We could no longer leave Lance's containment to chance or my bad judgment. Fencing the yard was an expense we could barely afford, but we agreed that a fence would in equal parts protect the public from Lance and Lance from the public, and protect us from lawsuits. It was doubtful that Lance would happily run himself ragged in an enclosed area, even one well over three quarters of an acre in size. But, when I wasn't up to walking him deep in the woods, anything was better than dealing with his unpredictability inside the house or letting him run free outside it.

The fence cost almost five thousand dollars, in part because Lance's jumping skills called for an additional foot of height. Purchasing such an expensive fence was a luxury that Lance had turned into a necessity.

We never did find out who made that call.

-31-

Devil Dog

There is a stigma that comes with owning a dog that bites. People in general tend not to care if the dog is nasty by nature or nurture. Family members in particular feel you care more about a lunatic canine than them.

Bad news travels especially fast on a cul-de-sac. After arriving on Oak Tree Drive, it didn't take long before our dog became quite a celebrity. One neighbor told me Lance even had his own nickname on the street—the Terminator. How cute. Unfortunately, he had earned it.

Neighbors viewed our dog as a menace and our property as off-limits. Jim, our next door neighbor, already had an opinion about everything else and he jumped at the chance to have one about Lance: "That dog is nuts, was from day one. That's why the other owners kept him outside. They were scared shitless. If you keep him (*you'd have to be crazier than that mutt if you do*) you better keep him outside too."

We severely restricted our dog's contact with other people. Although Clara and I mutually agreed to put up with Lance's insanity, we wouldn't volunteer anyone else for such a perilous assignment. We never trusted him with family, friends, visitors, or complete strangers. This dog was capable of biting anyone at any time, his owners included. The scant times we had a leashed Lance in public, people were warned not to approach him. Some would anyway ("Oh, he's so adorable!"), at times even briefly petting him before we could intervene. Lance, always the unpredictable one, never attacked anyone in those situations.

Two small fringe benefits: as our dog's reputation spread, the number of door-to-door salespeople and political campaigners dwindled to zero. We also saved a bundle in candy purchases at Halloween, as kids eliminated our house from their rounds. No treat was worth the possible trick (Lance).

Apparently, Lance was not troubled by his owners' and his own less than desirable reputations. He seemed intent on reinforcing them.

One time, my stepson Rob was up from Maryland. For two days, Lance ignored him. On the third day, out of the blue, he began growling at Rob while he was standing and conversing in the living room. When he got back to Maryland, Rob called Clara and said, "Mom, if you don't get rid of that dog, I'm coming back up there and get rid of him for you!"

On another occasion, we had family over for dinner. After eating, the men were in the living room watching football on television. I let our dog into the house to see if he would behave. After scanning the room he singled out Kevin, a nephew-in-law, walked over to him, sat down facing him, and began growling. Lance was immediately banished to the porch and stayed there until all our visitors had left. Every once in a long while, we'd give Lance such a test, a chance to prove himself. Invariably, he'd fail and back outside he'd go until all guests were gone.

Judy, Clara's sister, came up from Texas to visit one summer. A pattern quickly developed. Whenever she sat down in the living room, Lance would not let her get up. While sitting, the slightest movement on Judy's part, even curling her toes, elicited growls. We had to distract Lance or put him outside in order for Judy to regain her freedom of movement. Judy stopped visiting us.

Then, there was the time Angelo, a pest control technician, stopped by to inspect and chemically treat our house. For safety purposes, Lance was let out into our fenced backyard, while the inside of our house was treated. Subsequently, Angelo entered the basement via its outside entrance. I began reading the morning newspaper over a cup of coffee. Five minutes into the sports section, my concentration was broken by the devil dog's unmistakable bark. I hurried outside just in time to see Angelo, pesticide tank and all, leaping over our fence with Lance in hot pursuit. After leaving the basement, he had inadvertently entered the fenced portion of our yard where Lance was lying in wait. Thank God, Angelo was one of his company's younger and more agile employees. He assured me the whole thing was no big deal. For the record, Angelo never came back to inspect our house.

I cannot forget Andy, the home improvements man. Andy and his helper Mike were in the process of building a deck along the front of our house. The entire job went on for several weeks. One day, with the job nearing completion, Andy went inside to use the bathroom. Clara was on the new deck admiring the quality of the construction and discussing a further project with Mike. I was in our garage.

Andy entered the house through the front door. There soon followed a loud, vicious growl. Rushing inside, we found Andy, blood running down one hand, using his other to hold Lance securely by his collar. Lance was sitting upright and panting heavily, inexplicably allowing the man he had just bitten to physically restrain him. I took my dog by the collar (nervously, I might add) so Andy could let go and exit the house. Andy had ignored our warning not to enter the house before we let Lance out into the backyard. Outside, he told me, "It's my own fault. I shouldn't have gone inside alone. I should've let Clara go in first." Little did Andy know, had Clara or I gone into the house ahead of him, our dog might very well still have attacked him. Clara cleaned and bandaged Andy's wound. Fortunately, Lance was up to date with his rabies/distemper shots.

Although Andy told me not to worry about anything, after that day Mike did the rest of the work on our house by himself. As a former New Yorker, I instinctively assume everybody thinks in a litigious manner. For weeks, I expected to receive an ominous letter from a liability attorney representing Andy. It never happened. He was a man of his word, and there were never any legal proceedings. I had a friend in Pennsylvania.

Considering he was a biter, Lance's behavior at times left us mystified. One day, he got loose in our neighborhood. We were out looking for him, hoping and praying to find him before *he* found someone else. We were sitting on our front steps resting up in order to reinitiate the search when John, who lived two houses away, walked into our driveway with Lance in tow.

"I just came home from work. I found your dog lying in my yard."

Maybe he hadn't heard about Lance's reputation. He may have thought he had a dog by his collar, but we knew he really had a tiger by the tail.

What could I say? After apologizing, I quickly took Lance off his hands. Clara and I both breathed a huge sigh of relief. Lance had let a stranger forcibly walk him, by his collar no less.

There seemed to be neither rhyme nor reason to Lance's behavior. Whatever his rationale for biting, only Lance would ever know it. It was suggested our dog might be schizophrenic and in need of therapy. The search for a dog shrink was never made. I was skeptical about the idea of paying money, probably a lot of money, to have a human psychoanalyze our dog. Besides, I couldn't picture Lance staying put on a couch for anywhere near the typical one-hour therapy session.

Were we irresponsible, even selfish, dog owners? We had a dog that had to be constantly kept away from people and dogs. Sometimes we had to keep *ourselves* away from him. Friends told us they would, and we should, get rid of Lance, that he was a menace. We were told that euthanization would be the humane thing to do. I never bothered to debate the point. My head told me they might be right, but my heart told me "No way!"

Why did we continue living with a dog capable of attacking us, or anyone else, at any moment? Clara and I were on a mission. We were determined to give Lance whatever time he needed to overcome his damaged condition. Besides, there was a softer side to Lance. Quarantined because of his behavior, we were the only ones around our dog long enough to witness him at his best. Others never saw the Lance we did—playful, frisky, sometimes even, by all appearances, relaxed. He had an upbeat side that only we were aware existed: his Aztec Side-step dance, hanging out with our cats, happily greeting us when we came home, energetically busting my chops for a walk. Even more profound: every once in a while Lance's fanatical stare gave way to an intensely warm, gentle gaze. If a dog's eyes can talk, I'd swear his were saying *"Thank you for taking me in."*

The Schmidts had pushed Lance this close to being fit for extermination. Try as they might have, they had never totally destroyed his spirit. What Clara and I knew, and others didn't, was that Lance had plenty of Dr. Jekyll to go along with Mr. Hyde. Was our dog's upside worth his downside? We agreed it was, especially since his downside had been beaten into him.

Should we have had Lance destroyed? I don't know. We just couldn't do it.

-32-

Back Biter!

One summer the local area was battered with rain nearly every day. Water levels were extremely high throughout the area. On a boiling hot but rare rainless afternoon, I took Lance for a walk along a nearby trail in the midst of game lands. Being summertime, we weren't likely to become any hunter's targets.

Getting there required a very brief car ride. Not so brief that Lance didn't go bonkers in the car, but brief enough so that I didn't have to put up with his antics for too long.

After parking the car and letting Lance out, we began the hike which, at its inception, was all uphill. It was worth taking because I knew there would be a reward halfway up the hill: a stream that, thanks to the recent rains, figured to be full to overflowing. Though Lance loathed baths, he was a sucker for all the kinds of water found in nature; I was too. Whenever spotting a waterfall, pond, stream, etc., we both were sure to get soaked, sometimes even in bitterly cold weather. In that respect, Lance and I were birds—or dog and man—of a feather.

After a grueling walk in ninety-plus heat, I spotted the cross bridge that signaled we had reached the stream. Lance was panting heavily, his tongue hanging slack. He quickly lapped up the water I gave him from my canteen. Then, we walked down to the stream's bank. Sure enough, the water was extremely high and fast flowing.

I started untying my sneakers. Lance, of course, didn't need to disrobe so he hopped right in. After walking out to the deepest point, he stood in place and began working on his peace of mind in the rushing water. Having shed my sneakers, socks, T-shirt, and eyeglasses, I waded out to meet him. The comfortably cool water was a welcome relief from the day's excessive heat.

I lay down and submerged myself, leaving only my face out of the water. Lance was next to me, standing perfectly still, enjoying the water's relaxing effect. He remained there, the picture of tranquility, until his inherent restlessness got the best of him and he walked back to shore to begin a sniff-athon on dry land. I remained lying in the stream enjoying its soothing powers. The water was so calming, I became drowsy and closed my eyes. Ah, peace...

Lance soon took care of my drowsiness and my peace. He began barking. I opened my eyes, lifted my head out of the water, and looked onshore in his direction. *Did he want me out of the water? Sure. That's it. He was ready to continue hiking. Although a dog in name, he was really a work horse.*

Lance continued barking, staring straight at me while feverishly scurrying along the shoreline. This was not his usual "let's get back to walking" bark. This was a brand-new look for Lance. He looked possessed, but even more possessed than he usually looked when he looked possessed. Thoughts started flying at me like bullets: *This time he's really lost it; he's not coming back from this one. He doesn't even know who I am. I'm now on his enemies list right next to the Schmidts. What if he comes into the water charging at me? Me, climbing up a tree to get away from my own damn dog* (I started scanning for a suitable limb). *Here I am in the middle of nowhere with a dog that has gone mad. Forget about leashing him. I wouldn't even dare to get in the car with him, not in his condition. I'll have to make a run for it and just leave him here. Now he is going to have to be put down for sure. All our work has been for nothing—absolutely nothing.* It's amazing the kind of thinking that this dog and my imagination could generate.

Then, it dawned on me that he was barking, not growling, at me. Maybe he had spotted someone or something he thought worthy of my attention. I decided to look behind me.

Snake eyes! I found myself eyeball to eyeball with a snake whose head was poking out of the water, no more than a few feet away from me. I'm no expert on snake species, but, even had I been, without my glasses it's doubtful I could have determined what type it was. I did know copperheads, poisonous and native to the area, have elliptical eyes, unlike round-eyed nonpoisonous snakes. Having extremely poor vision, I'd have to be kisser-to-kisser with the snake in order to determine the shape of his eyes. I hadn't the slightest interest in conducting that type of close-up investigation. What I *was* interested in was getting my butt safely out of that stream.

There I was, well within the snake's striking distance. Something told me such a strike would be more likely if I scrambled rather than eased myself away from him. That in mind, I slowly put distance between us by using my hands and feet on the streambed to inch myself towards the shore. During my move towards land, I touched some very strange stuff on the stream's bottom, but this was no time to be squeamish.

What was the snake doing? Not eager to find out, I didn't look back at him. You know, that "ignorance is bliss" thing.

When the water was shallow enough for me to stand up and run in, that's exactly what I did, hustling up onto dry land where Lance waited with wagging tail. After putting my glasses on, I looked back into the water for the snake. There was none to be seen. Where could he be? No reason to wait around for an answer. It was time to grab my belongings and exit stage left.

I had completely misread my dog. Lance hadn't flipped out. Rather, what he did was save me from a snake bite or two.

Although the two of us would return to hike on this trail, only Lance ever entered the stream again.

-33-

Anna's Regret

Once we had moved to Canadensis, Anna occasionally called on us to see how Lance was doing, often bringing dog food and treats. Once, when neither of us was at home, she left several hundred dollars in an envelope to help defray a portion of a veterinary bill. During another visit, Lance did his best to make Anna feel right at home; he growled at her when she began petting him.

During one of her stops at our house, a lengthy conversation ensued. Anna finally admitted that over the years she had been bitten by Lance on multiple occasions, still only when, according to her, she had "touched a sore spot." Her sore spot alibi just might have some legs to it. With that first veterinary report in mind, my guess is that during the first ten years of his life, Lance was constantly loaded with sore spots (aka wounds from assaults). It probably would have been impossible for her to avoid touching one, no matter where she petted him. The good news? Those sore spots were a thing of the past. The bad news? Lance was still biting.

Though alleging she never personally witnessed any of his battles, Anna acknowledged Lance had to constantly fight off threats to his food supply. Those threats, coming from wild animals native to the area like foxes, coyotes, and bears, led to what she called countless scrapes that left Lance bloody and battered. To prevent such attacks, Anna got in the habit of sitting with Lance when he ate. Of course, he wouldn't always finish all his food in her presence, so this system was not fail-safe. She talked to the Schmidts about building him a large cage for protection, but it never happened.

Anna couldn't be with Lance day and night. When she wasn't, she did her best not to dwell on what might be going on in his life.

"I was so afraid to visit him after a while. It seemed like every time he was just about healed from one wound, there was a new one. I kept thinking that one day I'd show up and find him dead, and I knew I'd never forgive myself." Anna admitted that her well-intentioned hard work had left Lance at the mercy of sickos, other animals, and harsh weather, but she "just didn't know what else to do."

We never gave Anna the details of Lance's initial medical examination. There seemed no point. She knew what he'd been through.

She still hesitated to call the Schmidts anything more than "incompetent" and "uncaring" dog owners. She had her opinion and I had mine.

During a subsequent visit, I asked Anna how she had gotten involved in Lance's life. She put it succinctly: "You feel sorry for a dog, you start caring for it, the dog starts to depend on you, and you would feel guilty if you stopped." That's pretty much same process that got Clara and me so involved in his life.

Her last visit, sometime in 2004, turned out to be exceptionally emotional. In the middle of a light conversation, Anna began second-guessing herself out loud for not having taken Lance into her home immediately, when he was still a puppy and not yet so unruly. She deeply regretted what had happened to him as a result of being forced to live outside. She also had developed a dimmer view of the Schmidts.

"I remember when Lancie had to go to the hospital. Ted, that's Jack's oldest son, really threw him into their pickup truck. He did it right in front of me. He didn't care. It hurt so much to watch it, but I didn't, couldn't say how I felt. I just couldn't. I always felt Lance would pay if I said something."

"Another time, maybe I told you already, one time I showed up to take Lancie for a walk. Jack was out, heading away from the doghouse. He had a golf club. He looked mad about something; he usually is. He told me he'd just cleaned up the poop. Come on, with a golf club? Besides, I was the only one that did that job. When I got to the doghouse there was shit, poop everywhere. Who was he kidding? I couldn't coax Lance out of his doghouse. He always greeted me, and he *always* pestered me to go for a walk, but not this time. I felt uneasy leaving him there that day, but what else could I do? I guess you can put two and two together. I didn't then, or maybe I just didn't want to. I had my head stuck in the sand, or somewhere else if you know what I mean."

Anna continued. "Sometimes I wish I'd have taken Lancie into my house right away. I tried one time when he was a couple of years old. Inside, he was like a wild animal. He actually scared me. I guess it was already too late for him. He went after my cat and then started to fight my dog. Ed and I had to separate them. He bit Ed. I took him back to his place, right in the middle of a big snowstorm. I hated leaving him alone like that. I just keep wondering… if I had taken him in right away…"

She burst into tears. Clara and I did our best to console her.

After Anna collected herself, I asked, "Did you ever try again?"

"No, I don't think so."

I suggested to her that there was no guarantee that the Schmidts, as flaky as they were, would have allowed her to have Lance. After all, they had balked at letting me take him. The Schmidts were very possessive about their "property," even a dog they had no interest in. Clara tried to reassure Anna that she had made a superhuman effort to give Lance the best life possible under the circumstances. Without her sacrifices there would not have been a Lance for Clara and me to rescue.

There was one question I never asked Anna. Why had she for so long minimized his tendency to bite? My guess is she didn't want to jeopardize his chances of getting rescued by us.

No doubt we didn't convince Anna to let go of her remorse. I could, however, sense her relief knowing that Lance had at long last found a better place to live. That had been her wish all along. Her work was done.

-34-

Guilt Trip

Anna had her remorse and I had mine.

First there was the matter of the three years I had lived in Mount Bethel prior to meeting Lance. During the first few months there, whenever I jogged by the Schmidt property, Lance rushed up the lawn, pulling on his run and barking energetically at me as I ran by. Passing him on my way back home, he would much less enthusiastically watch me. Figuring his situation was none of my business, I inadvertently was rejecting Lance every time I didn't acknowledge him. Eventually, he stopped greeting me, not even bothering to come out of his doghouse. He had given up on me, and who could blame him? Why should he have kept wasting energy on a lost cause? He probably added me to his already lengthy list of lost causes. Now, belatedly, I realized what he had been trying to say to me: *Hey! Look at me! Take me with you.* It eats at me thinking how long I, like so many others, ignored him. Although his being isolated on the Schmidt property seemed senseless to me (why go to the trouble of having a dog just to keep it away from you?) and heartless, I assumed his owners weren't breaking any laws. His situation bothered me, and I left it at that. Then, after meeting him, why had I disregarded the message Lance was trying so hard to send me when he broke loose and showed up at my front door, not once but twice? Thanks to my inaction, Lance might very likely have finished off a miserable life with a violent, premature death, right down the road from me.

I glanced over at Lance, across the room, lying in front of the fireplace. He must have picked up on my thoughts. He had that all-knowing stare fixed on me. He didn't utter a word, yet I read him loud and clear. *Why did you go by my doghouse all those months, years really, and never stop for me? Think of all the walks we missed out on. I bet you're sorry.*

He was right.

-35-

More Lance-isms

Lance was detail oriented. He learned to distinguish the unique sounds of both Clara's car and mine as either approached home. He'd station himself next to our usual door of entry and wait attentively. Our dog sensed the impending arrival of either vehicle long before it could be seen or heard by any mere mortal.

My ritual after coming home from work was to relax for a bit with a snack while watching some television. Coming home from other than work was a different matter; off we'd go on a walk without delay. Lance developed rituals of his own. When I came home from my job, he'd already be lying next to my recliner waiting for me to begin my snack/TV routine. Arriving from other than work, he'd be waiting near the side door, ready to exit with me for a walk. Had he figured out my work schedule? Or was he just psychic? Beats me.

Lance never ate kibble out of any kind of dish. Perhaps this was a result of having had to eat sometimes spoiled, often bug-infested food from a dish for so many years at the Schmidts' place. He only ate dry food if it was spread out on the living room carpet. He might ignore the kibble for days and then eat all of it at once in a feverish binge. Since Lance was often getting Clara's home cooking, kibble was a distant second choice for him anyway.

We had the bathtub removed and replaced with a step-in shower. Every once in a while Lance would invite himself into the shower with Clara or I. This from the same dog that balked at being bathed by any human. Lance loved water, but only on his terms.

One morning, days after purchasing a pet bed for our cat, we found Lance attempting to cram himself into it. Clara and I had a good laugh watching our dog contort himself in an effort to fit into a cat-sized bed. Lance was silently telling us, *I want one of these too.* His tactic worked. Within days, he had his own doggie-sized bed.

Photos of Border Collies often show one or both of their ears limp or semi-limp, but both fully upright when the dog is on high alert. In a few pictures, the dog sports one upright ear and one semi-upright ear. Lance had an even more unique set of ears—one that he could raise and lower, the other always lying totally limp. It gave him a cute appearance. Unfortunately, he may have gotten this look the hard way. Back in his Mount Bethel days, his right ear had been sliced in half during a skirmish with an unknown assailant. It was stitched back together but, following surgery, may have lost all its "perkability." After examining many photos of other Border Collies, I still couldn't be sure if his right ear lay naturally limp or had been permanently disabled.

We spent a small fortune on designer dog toys for Lance's first Christmas with us. How did he show his appreciation? By completely ignoring the gifts and instead entertaining himself by ripping all the wrapping paper to shreds. It turned out our dog enjoyed tearing up any kind of paper. I often crumbled the pages of the daily newspaper and threw them to Lance. He'd immediately get down to the business of ripping each ball into a million pieces. Having learned our dog had such simple tastes made subsequent Christmases a lot less costly.

One morning Clara woke me up and said, "You'd better come see what Mr. Lancie has done." I had been collecting *Runner's World* magazines with the intention of eventually cutting out and saving the most informative articles re: running, nutrition, stretching, and exercising. The magazines were kept in a neat pile next to my recliner. When I entered the living room, there was Lance putting the finishing touches on the *very last* magazine. All the others had already been thoroughly and neatly shredded as if by a mechanical paper cutter. Lance seemed quite proud of his work. I attempted to reassemble the magazines, but soon gave up. This dog had absolutely no consideration.

CAN I HAVE ONE OF THESE?

MISSION ACCOMPLISHED

-36-

Lance Goes Batty

Whether on our walks or just hanging out at home, I often conversed with Lance. I did most of the talking. On second thought, I did all the talking, probably because Lance was such a great listener.

One evening late at night, I was relaxing in the living room reading a book. Lance lay on the floor facing me with his head drooped over the edge of his pillow.

Time for a little heart-to-heart.

"Are you a good dog?"

Lance looked at me quizzically.

"When are you going to stop biting Mommy?"

He began to perk up.

"We're trying our best to make you feel at home. It'd be nice if you'd make a better effort to show some gratitude."

He lifted his head and tilted it to one side. I knew he was paying attention. Maybe he might give me some feedback.

"You know how your mom and dad feel about you, or don't you?"

Lance slowly stood up, stretched, and began to amble over to me. As he drew nearer, up went my anxiety level. *Now look what I've gotten myself into!* Which Lance was approaching me? Tail wagging at full tilt (of course, his wagging tail was indicative of absolutely nothing) he reached me and put his chin on my knee. He stood at a right angle to me. This wasn't such a safe setup for petting Lance—there really wasn't any—so I decided that for the time being I'd simply continue talking.

"You're a good boy, yes, you are."

Acting like any dog would, he remained in expecting-to-be-petted mode. Since I was dealing with Lance, there was the little matter of getting over the fear of being bitten.

In the midst of deciding what to do next, I was distracted by a fluttering sound and looked up to see a bird flying near the ceiling. I had no idea how or when he'd entered the scene but, up to this point, he had managed to escape being detected by Lance. Perhaps my dog was too engrossed in our conversation.

The bird began swooping throughout the living room. Spotting it, Lance made several unsuccessful attempts to grab it with his mouth as it flew by.

The bird landed on the floor.

There was something un-birdlike about this creature's behavior. I got up and walked over to get a better look at it. That's when I realized it was in fact a bat, this being the closest I'd ever been to one in my lifetime. Picture your basic mouse with wings, sort of. Again taking flight, it occasionally stopped to latch onto this or that wall, until finally it came to rest again on the living room floor, planting itself with wings fully spread open.

Lance was by now beside himself. He cautiously danced around the bat, barking at the top of his lungs, uncertain how to handle the mysterious creature lying in front of him. Then, determined to herd this winged enigma, Lance assumed the classic Border Collie crouch, circling his "flock," a flock that consisted of one apparently disinterested and unimpressed winged mammal. All my dog's fevered activity left the bat unmoved—literally. He remained frozen in place on the floor. Would Lance attack and I soon be watching some kind of grotesque dog versus bat duel? The thought of either of us contracting rabies or some such thing also ran through my mind. Lance, at least, was up to date on his shots; I certainly wasn't.

Lance didn't let up. He kept circling the bat, letting out some of the highest pitched howls I'd ever heard. Though sounding unearthly to me, they left the bat unfazed and motionless.

I yelled to Clara, already in bed, "There's a bat in the house!" and rushed into the computer room. Googling "how to get bats out of your house", I waited impatiently for a response. No time for professional assistance; something had to be done right away. I checked out a do-it-yourself site. Per instructions, I opened the living room windows and both the front and side doors. Clara, who had armed herself with a broom, turned off the inside lights. It was early winter and the house quickly chilled with all the extra ventilation. Of course, at this particular moment getting this beast out of the house was far more important than keeping warm.

The four of us remained in the pitch-black living room. Then, just as promised on the website, the bat headed outdoors. Lance followed it and then came back inside, full of self-importance, acting as if *he* had chased it away. Clara and I knew better. We were pretty certain he hadn't been able to make heads or tails out of that strange critter.

Another thing was for certain. It was time to get my eyeglass prescription adjusted.

-37-

Beast of Burden

Late fall. A Sunday night. A little after 9:00 p.m. It was dark, even darker because of an overcast sky. Lance and I were already well into our 2,456th hike (or was it our 2,457th?).

This was going to be a short stroll no matter what Lance thought. The New York Giants were on TV tonight. I had watched the first half of the game. I planned to take a short walk with Lance during halftime and get back home in time to see most of the second half.

About fifteen minutes had passed since we started our jaunt. I turned around and began heading for home, upping my pace. This way there'd be plenty of game left by the time we got to the house.

As was his custom, Lance had wandered off by himself, presumably keeping me on his radar and, therefore, aware of my about-face. I expected him to come charging up from behind me. It didn't happen. Where was he? I continued on by myself, confident that at any moment my dog would catch up with me.

Then, from way off in the distance behind me, came a series of barks followed by an eerie silence. I called out for Lance to come. Nothing. Again I called. Dead quiet. I made a 360° turn, flashlight in hand. No dog. The woods were pitch-black and still. Several more "Here Lance(s)!" brought nothing but their own echoes. I started backtracking.

Had I let my dog loose in the woods one time too many? Would I have to begin a painful search for a dead dog? Would I be able to scare off his attacker or would I be its next victim? If I survived, would I have to carry Lance all the way home so scavengers couldn't pick at his body? Fear and guilt twisted my stomach into a pretzel.

How devastated Clara would be. She loved him even though he terrified her. Would she blame me? Yes, she would. She would be madder at me for letting this happen then she was at Lance for all the times he had bitten her. I wanted to make a deal with a higher power so He or She would undo what I feared had happened.

An ominous silence surrounded me. I was unsure what to do next: begin a potentially dangerous search for Lance in the dark of night or go home empty-handed. Neither alternative appealed to me. I stood immobile on the trail, unable to decide on my next move.

All at once the quiet was broken by heavy breathing coming from behind me. My heart stopped. What, or who, was it?

I whirled around and was relieved to see Lance, not some four-legged or two-legged monster, appear from behind a large boulder. He was still alive! My sense of relief was quickly replaced with curiosity. He had what looked to be a bunch of straw in his mouth. What in the world had this dog gotten into? He approached, panting furiously.

Not being a country boy by birth, it took me a bit longer than the average northern Pennsylvanian to realize what had happened. Lance had met up with a porcupine and was sporting a mouthful of quills. And they say Border Collies are so smart!

After leashing him, I decided to try walking home on paved roads rather than backtrack through the dark woods. I could see car lights going by some fifty or so yards north of us, so we headed in that direction.

Lance was a mess, we were miles from home, and I had no cell phone. There was nothing to do but to keep walking. To top things off, just as we began the journey home, it started to rain.

Reaching Bear Town Road, we proceeded in the direction of home, some four miles away. I kept my dog on a very short leash as parts of the road had extremely narrow shoulders and were very winding. Visibility was also limited as we were now in the midst of a heavy downpour and a lentil soup-like fog. A few passing cars sped by dangerously close to us.

As we walked, I tried to give Lance some words of encouragement. Of course, what exactly can you say to make a dog feel better when he's suffering with a mouthful of porcupine quills? To add to the excitement, somewhere along the way the flashlight punted.

We made a left onto Route 447 and plodded on, both of us thoroughly soaked.

Lance was gasping for air. The effort he had to put into each breath convinced me he was dangerously exhausted and might choke to death. We were still over a mile from home. I couldn't leave Lance alone and come back for him with my car. On the other hand, I wasn't sure he could make the final lap home in the condition he was. *Why oh why hadn't I taken my cell phone with me!?*

There was only one thing to do—pick Lance up and carry him the rest of the way. Did I have the strength and endurance? More to the point, did I have the nerve? Time to find out. Coming to a stop, I stuffed the leash handle into my jacket pocket, bent down, took a deep breath and nervously cradled Lance with my arms under his belly. Up he went, all sixty-five pounds of him. Although my face was now within striking distance for his teeth, if he went after me he had way too many quills in his mouth to bite anything. However, if he lunged at me and if porcupine needles were sharp on both ends, I'd get stuck with quite a few. To my great relief, Lance was far too preoccupied with his own discomfort to bother threatening me. He wasn't even up to growling.

Having passed the fear test, I now had to deal with the challenge of carrying Lance the rest of the way home. Getting a car ride from a Good Samaritan was unlikely. Traffic was extremely light and not one driver of those passing by stopped to offer a ride. Maybe they couldn't see us. Or maybe Lance's reputation was that widespread. Then again, possibly *I* looked the lunatic, soaked to the bone and carrying a dog in a dark mixture of rain and fog, sans flashlight.

We, or rather I, staggered on. Lance's dead weight eventually took its toll; my lower (bad) back began aching.

Reaching a spot where two large rocks sat just off the road, I walked over to one and plopped my weary bones on it, letting Lance lie on my lap. He continued his mixture of panting and gasping. Was he in shock? I wondered if the quills were toxic. My knowledge of porcupines was woefully lacking.

After a brief respite, I resumed walking, still carrying my wounded companion.

I was never so glad to see the intersection of Route 447 and Oak Tree Drive. Just to make this walk even more enjoyable, the last hundred yards were uphill.

Clara, with umbrella and flashlight, was waiting on the front deck. She had wanted to start a search for us, but had no idea where to begin looking.

Once in the house, I could finally lay my heavy burden down. Collapsing into a chair, I asked Clara to bring me a pair of pliers in order to initiate quill removal. She let out a hearty laugh and I quickly got the joke. What was I thinking? Imagine trying to get a dog, especially one with Lance's temperament, to sit still while having countless porcupine needles painfully extracted from his mouth.

Because this was an after-hours emergency, we were faced with taking an ever-so-rare car trip with Lance to the Chambers Animal Hospital, the only game in town that late in the night. Would its personnel lift their ban and treat Lance? I called ahead and explained to the receptionist that my dog had been "porcupined." She recognized the name Lance and half-jokingly said, "We'll have the muzzle ready." I shot back, "Don't think you'll need it."

While I drove, Clara, forced against her wishes to ride in a car with the dreaded devil dog, sat in the back seat simultaneously attempting to control and comfort our canine pincushion. Even with all those needles, Lance was his typical self, barking in between gasps and lunging at each set of passing car headlights. Lance had a mouthful and Clara had her hands full.

While likely not delighted to see Lance, no doubt the hospital employees were at least relieved to see his mouth incapacitated.

Quill removal went on well into the night.

Thankfully, by the following morning, my back had recovered from the previous night's endurance contest. I drove to the hospital to pick up the patient, wondering what kind of condition Lance would be in.

To my surprise, he showed no ill effects from his previous night's ordeal. In fact, he was sufficiently energized to make the car ride back home the usual adventure.

The hospital charged two dollars per quill. Despite the fact the final count came to well over two hundred quills, including those in his nostrils and ears, there was no wholesale discount. In addition, since this emergency care was provided after normal clinic hours, there was an extra fee. Apparently, this particular escapade of Lance's cost me more financially than it cost him physically.

As for the Giants, I never got to see them lose (Washington 22— New York 10).

How do you spell "Lance"? N-e-v-e-r-a-d-u-l-l-m-o-m-e-n-t!

-38-

The Many Moods of Lance

Aggressive streak:

When Lance wasn't menacing man or dog, he found ways to keep himself busy with other animals. On one of our walks, he caught and killed an adult deer, a horrible sight and something, despite my attempts, I was powerless to stop. Lance was completely bestial. All the way back home I kept thinking, *And we're living with this wild animal in our house?* On another occasion, he caught and ate a woodchuck, a meal his digestive system didn't take kindly to, necessitating a trip to the vet. Then, there was that porcupine. Lance may have been a victim of circumstance, but it wouldn't surprise me if he was the one who initiated the confrontation.

Defensive streak:

One day while walking a leashed Lance, we were confronted by a trio of Boxers on the loose in an open field. All three began alternately charging at my dog and then backing off. Lance, too busy defending himself, would not retreat with me. If I unleashed him, all hell would break loose, yet keeping him restricted on his leash put Lance at a danger-ous disadvantage. Fearing a massacre, I joined in, yelling and charging at Lance's attackers, hoping to drive them away. My attempts failed, leaving me surrounded by four sets of snarling teeth. Lance was keeping these dogs at bay, but for how much longer? Fortunately, I wouldn't have to find out. Coming out of nowhere, a man grabbed two of the Boxers by the collar and ran off with them. The third one followed. This man never said a word to me and I was never to see him or his dogs again.

Passive streak:

Lance was a high-strung, predatory animal. Add his defensive ag-gressiveness and you had an extremely volatile mix. The same dog that suffered severe panic attacks was just as likely to fearlessly confront all kinds of living creatures, even those many times his size. Yet, this dog was an absolute marshmallow around, of all things, a rather easy target—cats.

For a while, Lance had had a stray gray tabby as a bunk mate while living on the Schmidts' property. Anna often found Lance and his feline friend sleeping inside his doghouse. She noticed that at mealtime, until he had finished eating out of his bowl, he wouldn't let the cat eat from it. This meant there were days when there'd be no food left for the cat. Anna solved that problem by providing the cat with a separate dish of food, which a well-mannered Lance didn't touch. However, until Lance was done eating from his own bowl, he would not allow the cat to begin eating from his designated dish; Lance's growling saw to that. Did Lance have control issues? If so, his feline friend accepted such behavior because the two were a team for well over a year.

One day the cat was gone. Coincidentally, when Clara and I were still living in Mount Bethel, my stepson Rob found a gray cat living among the garbage cans alongside our apartment building. He took this cat back home with him to Maryland and named it Scout. Scout lives and prospers to this day. Had Scout been Lance's bunk mate?

If ever there was a cat tailor-made for a dog to dislike, it was Ashley. Let me state unequivocally that Ashley was one obnoxious feline. From the first day we had him, he rarely hung out with us, preferring to stay outside or, if inside, keep his distance. He lived an asocial life, graciously allowing us to feed him. When Ashley wanted to come inside, he didn't meow. No, he aggressively banged on the screen door loud enough to be heard by neighbors.

Once in Canadensis, Ashley didn't change. He remained the same aloof, distant, egotistical feline he had always been—catty in all the ways that only a true cat lover could fully appreciate. If Lance had chased Ashley throughout our apartment in Mount Bethel with evil intent, in Canadensis he had daily opportunities to do him in. Instead, Lance ignored him. I'm sure he had sufficient time to size Ashley up as not being his kind of cat. He treated that critter as well as anyone could. Postscript: Ashley died in 2006 from terminal nastiness.

Another cat, Winky, undernourished and on his way to becoming feral, showed up at our front door a few months after we moved to Canadensis. Rather than resent this newcomer, Lance greeted him with open paws. Although we were always wary of our dog, Winky, black and white like Lance, had a much different relationship with him. This cat nonchalantly rubbed up against Lance's legs when they were standing next to each other. They often slept side by side. The two got along as if they had known each other for years. We figured the cat must be either fearless or clueless, but maybe he knew something about Lance. *This dog doesn't have any problems with me. I'm a cat. He has issues with bigger game—humans, dogs, and wild animals.*

When I'd take Lance outside on the leash, Winky had a little game he liked to play. Lying in wait as my dog and I headed out onto the street, he'd stalk us, walking parallel to us while hidden in the woods. Then he'd leap out onto the road, as if trying to startle us. Sometimes he'd briefly follow us when we headed into the woods. Then, like any self-respecting cat, he'd tire of the exercise and head back home.

Cats rarely seek out other people's dogs, but our neighbors' cats frequently visited Lance. When he was outside in the yard, it was not uncommon to find Lance resting on or under the steps, a cat or two sacked out with him.

One day we were taking a long, Lance-inspired hike through the woods that brought us near the south side of Bear Town Road, several miles away from our starting point. After turning around and taking the first steps homeward, the infamous black cat crossed our path, strolling out of the woods and stopping in front of us. He wore a collar and looked well fed, probably the pet of someone living nearby. I feared there might be a dog-chase-cat event that would take Lance into parts unknown, forcing me to follow him there. Fortunately, he didn't run, but rather walked up to the feline stranger, which for his part calmly awaited Lance's arrival. Tail wagging, Lance sniffed the cat in all the places a dog sniffs, the cat patiently waiting until the examination was over. When done, they rubbed noses. Then, just like that, the cat loped away and Lance and I resumed our walk home. Even felines that were complete strangers received a warm welcome from Lance.

I don't think Lance's gentle behavior around felines required self-control on his part. Like Winky, I believe he had a soft spot for cats. Why? Maybe it was just his nature. Then again, maybe it was because, unlike so many other living creatures, cats had never harmed him. Whatever the case, the irony was not lost on me. Clara and I were constantly on guard around our dog, while tabbies of all kinds knew they had nothing to fear when in Lance's company. He was the cat's meow. Make that the *cats'* meow.

Another possible example of Lance's softer side: one day while walking in the woods behind my house in Canadensis, we came upon a fawn that apparently had died. Kneeling beside it, I detected no movement or respiration. What really convinced me the young deer was no longer living was the fact that Lance showed little interest, though his potential victim was there for the taking. Just to be on the safe side, when we got back home, I called the local animal rescue hotline. The lady responding advised me the fawn was likely not dead. She said female deer teach their young to feign death when the latter are left by themselves. She suggested that, if I went back at day's end, the young deer would most likely be gone. I did and it was. Had Lance given a defenseless animal a break or had he been fooled like I was?

Protective Streak:

It was a late spring afternoon. I was at work, Clara was at home watching television, and Lance was resting on the living room floor. Lance sprang to his feet and began barking and pacing frenetically. Clara's immediate fear: *Is he going to come after me?* When it became clear he was reacting to something outside, Clara decided to let him into the yard so he could blow off steam. She opened the side door, but Lance refused to exit. Instead, he began scurrying from room to room inside the house, howling like a wolf. Clara walked out onto the side stoop and spotted a large brown bear roaming around in the backyard just a few feet away from her. Lance pounded on the screen door, as if wanting to get outside. However, when Clara opened the door, he hesitated. Lance might have been crazy, but he was no fool.

Clara wisely went back inside the house. She watched the bear from the safety of the closed screen door, holding the inside door just in case it too might have to be closed. The bear, in turn, stopped in his tracks and eyeballed her.

The next thing Clara knew, she heard Lance howling—from outside the house! She rushed to the living room and checked the front screen door. It was closed, but Lance must have opened it to get onto the front deck, either pulling the door latch down with his mouth, or pushing it down with his chin or paw(s). Whichever was the case, he shoved the door open and dashed out, letting the door close behind him. Positioned on the front deck, he barked nonstop at the top of his lungs, causing the bear to amble across the backyard, climb over fence, walk down the driveway, and continue into the woods.

Clara initially thought Lance's reluctance to leave the house was due to his fear of the bear. Later, she concluded that by refusing to go out, he had been trying to make *her* aware of the danger awaiting in the yard. When she made the mistake (in Lance's eyes) of stepping outside, he managed to get himself out the front door to drive the bear away. After all, when the curtain dropped on this scene, Clara was safely inside and it was Lance who was outside on the deck vocally prodding the bear to leave the premises. I agree with Clara's assessment. In all of the years spent with him, I only saw one creature make Lance cower—Mr. Schmidt—which says all you need to know about that "gentleman."

HOUNDED INTO A HIKE

WHO, LITTLE OLD ME?

LANCE AND FRIEND

WINKY RULES

DOG AT WORK

A JOB WELL DONE

OH, YOU WANTED TO READ THE PAPER?

DON'T EVEN THINK ABOUT TOUCHING MY BISCUIT

-39-

The Truth Hurts

IF A DOG CANNOT LIVE ACCORDING TO HIS INSTINCTS, HE
WILL USUALLY DEVELOP ABNORMAL BEHAVIOR.

– FROM AN INTERNET WEBSITE

More than three years into Project Lance and we were still waiting for this dog to straighten out. Until meeting Lance, I had always thought of a dog as an escape, a timeout from the business of life. A canine is the friendly, loyal family member that happens to have four legs. Not this one. Inside the house, nothing much had changed. Whenever he approached us, the increase in tension was as palpable as ever. Lights were still being kept on around the clock to prevent sneak attacks.

Lance hadn't bit Clara in a while, mainly because she kept her distance. Clara now only rarely let Lance take food dangling from her mouth and she didn't touch him at all anymore. She'd tried the "acting as if" thing for a while, but her heart was never really in it. She reasoned that Lance's continuing aggressive reaction to being petted showed that he, unlike a healthy dog, didn't enjoy being petted. It was in their mutual interest that she had decided to keep her hands off him, period. By this time, he'd transformed her into a nervous wreck. She admitted feeling a great sense of relief whenever I took him outside for a walk. When Lance and I returned home, her anxiety level shot right back up. I still ventured to pet Lance, but only rarely and briefly, and with eyes firmly fixed on his mouth. Luckily, I'd always managed to escape his snapping jaws.

Lance had been banned from mixing with the public long ago. We couldn't let people into the house without making absolutely certain he exited first. Outside, I let Lance walk into the deepest bowels of the Delaware State Forest and other nearby woods, not only because he enjoyed it, but also to minimize his chances of meeting people. We couldn't get a respite from him, because we'd never subject a dog-sitter to his lunacy.

The subject of euthanization had come up again some months earlier, but was quickly dropped. Clara and I still considered it an unacceptable option. We were in this thing with Lance for the long haul.

Was Lance making any progress at all? Every once in a while he still pinned himself against the wall in a state of panic, but he hadn't stood in a corner and growled at us for quite some time. In our minds, that counted for something. We rationalized his continuing misbehavior and celebrated the smallest sign that he might be improving, all the while harboring the nagging belief that he probably hadn't changed one iota.

This was not normal pet ownership. What was it? Acceptance? Resignation? Insanity? There's another expression in the recovery field: "the elephant in the living room." It refers to the problem staring a household in the face —the family addict and his negative behavior— that, instead of being confronted, is tiptoed around. In our household, the "elephant" we tiptoed around was a sixty-five pound dog. All of our questions about him could be summed up in one: why hadn't he realized by now he was in a safe place?

I decided to take one more stab at researching the effects of abuse and neglect on dogs in general and, this time, on Border Collies in particular. Maybe, just maybe, there remained a stone unturned that was covering the secret to improving Lance's behavior. Taking my laptop and several relevant library books onto the porch, I sat down and began my study.

Four themes kept coming up in the books and on websites: a dog being forced to live outside, constantly being left in isolation, not getting enough exercise/training, and being subjected to physical abuse.

Common effects on dogs of:

1) Being forced to live outside:

I had always felt that keeping a dog outside 24/7 was proof positive that an owner wasn't really a dog lover. I found research that supported my suspicions. A dog condemned to live outside is at risk for hypothermia and frostbite in the winter and heatstroke in the summer, especially an older dog. In rainstorms, for some dogs thunder is painful; for all dogs, lightning is dangerous. A dog stuck outside day and night can more easily get injured/sick/infected and is less likely to get needed medical treatment in a timely fashion, if at all. If provided, food and water can quickly become unsanitary. Last, but far from least, a dog stuck outside is at the mercy of predators.

2) Being kept isolated:

In addition to the above-mentioned physical dangers inherent in forcing a dog to live outside, it automatically isolates him and starts a vicious cycle: having little or no opportunity to become socialized makes it much more likely he will fare poorly during any contact he might have with people or other domestic animals, which in turn increases the likelihood he will continue to be kept by himself.

A dog forced to live alone might even assume he has done something wrong and see isolation as his punishment.

Severe isolation can lead to symptoms of canine depression: withdrawal, reduced appetite, poor sleeping habits, excessive salivation, rapid heart rate, excessively high metabolic/respiratory rate, reduced urine output, walking slowly, and having less energy.

3) Getting insufficient exercise can lead to:

- Poor muscle tone
- Obesity
- Heart ailments
- Bone disorders
- Destructive digging, scratching, and chewing
- Unmanageable, unruly, and extremely hyper behavior
- Jumping up on people
- Irritability
- Insomnia
- Excessive barking/whining
- Rough playing, biting, or even predatory behavior

The term "kennel crazy" exists. It results from the combined effects of lack of exercise and isolation. As the name implies, it often refers to a dog that has been in a shelter for a lengthy period of time. It can also occur in dogs that are caged or tethered on a regular basis and to dogs continuously left alone. Symptoms include endless pacing (often seen in the big cats kept in a zoo), spinning in circles, chewing wood, metal, and even himself (were any of Lance's wounds self-inflicted?), fighting with inanimate objects, suffering panic attacks, and biting people.

Now for the Border Collie. The Border Collie thinks, learns, and acts like a dog, but like a certain kind of dog, one having the characteristics and behavior patterns specific to his breed. That said, being a Border Collie, Lance suffered his neglect and abuse in ways unique to his kind.

1A) *Being forced to live outside:*

Lance faced the same hazards as noted above for dogs in general and, as a Border Collie, he was especially vulnerable to the pain generated by loud noises. One book noted, "The Border Collie in particular, because of his hypersensitivity to noise, will probably go mad if left outside over a Fourth of July weekend." Lance had been stuck outside during ten Fourth of July weekends, and an equal number of hunting seasons in addition to innumerable thunderstorms.

2A) *Being kept isolated:*

The Border Collie does not like to be left by himself for more than a few hours. When alone, he quickly becomes bored and nervous. Separation anxiety is very common in this breed. During his years in Mount Bethel, Lance kept breaking off his run and showing up at Anna's place and then, after meeting me, at mine.

According to the American Kennel Club, the Border Collie can be distant around strangers, and it is critical to socialize this breed with both people and other dogs and cats at a young age to prevent behavior problems. Lacking socialization, he can become extremely shy, and his more typical reserved and standoffish demeanor around strangers can turn aggressive.

Isolation also deprives this breed of the training that it so desperately needs. For a Border Collie, training is not a luxury, but a necessity. Because of its high degree of intelligence, this dog requires regular mental stimulation in order to satisfy its curiosity and feel content. Without new experiences, the Border Collie stagnates. This is a strong-willed dog that, if untrained, will want to be in charge, make his own decisions, and react as he sees fit. In addition, if not kept busy mentally as well as physically, he can become over-reactive and sound sensitive beyond even the norm for his breed.

The Border Collie is an early and quick learner. The commands we taught Lance he could have easily mastered by the age of three months. I've watched TV shows and YouTube videos that featured Border Collies possessing extensive vocabularies and performing sophisticated tricks. I saw a live demonstration of a Border Collie's talents when we visited Karen O'Brien's dog training facility. All those dogs realized the same potential that Lance had been born with, but was never able to tap into. A dog born desperately needing a purpose grew up having none.

3A) Getting insufficient exercise:

Suited for herding and canine sports, the Border Collie needs huge amounts of exercise to curb his hyperactivity and stay happy. Couch-potato living just won't do for this breed. Lance's walks around the block with Anna must have seemed like a bad joke to him. According to the Border Collie Rescue Association, the question "How much exercise does a Border Collie require?" is unanswerable. A Border Collie kept as a domestic pet should be given at a minimum two to three hours of vigorous exercise daily to stave off potential problems like severe anxiety and destructive behavior. While it is virtually impossible to over-exercise a Border Collie, be advised he wouldn't let you know even if he were getting exhausted. Rest must be enforced because this is a dog that, if allowed, might exercise himself to death. Of course, overwork wasn't Lance's problem while on the Schmidt property. Quite the opposite—when not being assaulted, he vegetated.

A Border Collie that is not given enough exercise and/or is constantly confined in too small a space can develop chronic anxiety and destructive behaviors, and is especially prone to going kennel crazy. Anna told me that one day she arrived at the Schmidt property and found Lance "spinning like a top," and that he only stopped when she began talking to him.

Lance didn't have a sedentary bone in his body. He was built for activity, be it work or play. He was ten-years-old when I met him and still extremely energetic. For him to have been condemned to sleeping/killing time at the end of a run for so many years was a crime against his very nature.

4) Physical abuse:

This is an extreme form of maltreatment of any dog, regardless of breed. The following is a list of some, but by far not all, indicators that signal a dog might be living in an abusive situation. A **(Lance)** signifies which indicators were a documented part of Lance's experience:

1. The obvious signs are broken bones, burns, cuts and lacerations or odd markings like bruises or scars anywhere on the body. **(Lance)**
2. The dog has a lengthy history of injuries. **(Lance)**
3. The owner or keeper ignores or denies the injuries, doesn't seem to be able to explain them or downplays their seriousness. **(Lance)**

4. The owner is reluctant to provide treatment for the dog. As a result, some or all injuries may be poorly attended to or not attended to at all. **(Lance)**

5. The owner or caregiver is unusually harsh or aggressive towards the dog. **(Lance)**

6. The collar is kept abnormally tight.

7. The dog is kept in remote parts of the yard or house with very little social interaction. **(Lance)**

8. The dog shows behavior changes such as signs of being afraid around the abuser. He may be unusually subdued and submissive, cower, keep head down and/or tail between the legs or hide when the abuser comes into view. He may whimper or cry in fear when near the abuser. **(Lance)**

9. The dog overreacts to the presence of a particular object like a leash or stick. **(Lance)**

10. The dog shows signs of malnutrition, looks underweight, and is desperate for any crumb of food. He may look weak and lack in energy. He may bark obsessively out of hunger. (**Lance**, for several months during first year of his life).

11. He exhibits chained aggression or may bite in fear. **(Lance)**

12. The dog growls for unknown reasons in the presence of his owner or other people involved in the abuse. (**Lance?** I know he did in the presence of people not involved in his abuse).

13. The owner repeatedly has dogs that seem to die at a young age. **(Lance)**

14. The dog is subjected to attacks by animals and/or people in addition to the owner(s). **(Lance)**

The Border Collie is a highly intelligent dog, topping many lists as *the* most intelligent canine. He is also an emotional dog that reacts quickly and strongly to stimuli in his environment. He needs an owner who will spend a lot of time with him and provide constant, positive leadership, plus lots of training and exercise. In the right hands, this dog's combination of intelligence and sensitivity is a gift to be nurtured. However, in neglectful and abusive circumstances, the Border Collie is doomed to suffer an additional, deeper layer of psychological damage than many other breeds might. Although physically a very durable dog, a Border Collie is quite fragile emotionally. Like any canine, he reacts to violence with fear and loss of self-confidence. However, even lesser amounts of neglect or abuse can deeply impact this particular breed. What doesn't necessarily impress other breeds can sit especially deep with a Border Collie. He doesn't easily forget or take things in stride.

Having an especially strong need for love, structure, and fellowship, if a Border Collie cannot obtain these from his environment, he will try to withdraw from it. If withdrawal is impossible and his immediate surroundings become physically threatening, the panic attack is often the next line of defense for a Border Collie. Being very sensitive in nature, he tends to shut down if treated with a heavy hand. When corrected/ disciplined too harshly, he might become temporarily immobile.

The Border Collie can be high-strung and often is ready to engage in a battle of wits with his owner. "Never leave a Border Collie to his own devices," warns a website. "If the Border Collie feels shortchanged in the areas of mental and physical exercise, he can become a neurotic nuisance." The Border Collie Rescue Association describes him as "the fanatical black-and-white dog" that can be hyper and hard to handle. Border Collies can become rogue dogs and cross the line between herding and hunting, making them no longer trustworthy around children and livestock. Such dogs are usually exterminated. I got to thinking. Could Lance's disposition have less to do with nurture and more to do with nature? Would he have been the way he was no matter how he grew up? Was his behavior simply typical of a Border Collie gone bad? Did he belong to the lunatic fringe of his breed and, if so, had he been "born to be wild?" If so, why would anybody take a chance owning a dog of his breed?

Then, I came back to my senses. I remembered Mickey. The previous spring, Clara and I had gone to Stroudsburg, Pennsylvania and visited the Quiet Valley Living Historical Farm, styled after a nineteenth-century German farm. It was like entering a time tunnel. Tours were provided of rustic houses featuring handmade furniture. All the participants were dressed in the style of those earlier times. Some were demonstrating the use of olden farm tools, while others were making clothes by hand. Foods were prepared using the primitive cooking methods of the 1800s. There also was a herding demonstration involving a flock of sheep, a shepherdess, and two Border Collies, Mickey and Charlie. Prior to the demonstration, I asked the owner if her dogs were approachable. She assured me they were. In fact, she was letting them mingle freely with a large crowd of people. I was the only person on edge as I tentatively petted both, my guard up as the dogs were the spitting image of Lance. They then ran off to do their work with the sheep, entertaining an appreciative audience. Later in the day, I saw the dogs standing with their owner across a field from me. I called, "Mickey!" He turned, spotted me, and came flying over, his face beaming as if he was reuniting with a long-lost friend. I was looking at the kind of Border Collie Lance would never be. This was a dog that had been raised properly and whose energy and intelligence had been channeled into productive activity. He was everything that is right about a Border Collie. Lance and Mickey, Mickey and Lance. They were like identical twins separated at birth, destined to live such different lives. I can't help but believe that Mickey was the kind of dog Lance would have been had fate not treated him so cruelly.

Because he is such a complex, high maintenance, and demanding dog, constant companionship, sufficient training, and plentiful exercise are indispensable to raising a happy Border Collie. Even when living in the best of circumstances, he can be a handful. Since Lance had grown up in the worst of circumstances, we got what he already was, an adult dog with his wires crossed. So many of the Border Collie's noteworthy features—dynamism, acute reactivity to stimuli, heightened awareness of his surroundings, an analytical mind—were not cultivated, but rather distorted in Lance. How else to explain his excessive excitability, inappropriate responses to stimuli, defensive posturing, freezing up and fear biting?

I came away from my fact-finding mission with no new ideas for improving Lance's behavior. What I had gained was a deeper understanding of the damage that had been done to him, which, in turn, led to an even greater appreciation of the fact he was approachable at all.

-40-

A Tale of Two Survivors

"Hey, do you want to go Booby bye-bye?" Of course he did. Lance scrambled to his feet, I hooked him up to his leash and out the door we went. After rushing through the open gate and down the driveway, we crossed the street and headed into the woods. I let him loose and Lance immediately began doing what dogs do best, sniff everything in sight and, undoubtedly, some things out of sight.

Lance greeted all our walks with such fervor, you'd think each was his first ever. For my dog, exercise was fun to be enjoyed, not endured, and roaming in the woods was never boring. As for me, my mental wheels have a habit of working overtime and our hikes usually helped slow them down. Usually, but not so this day. This would turn out to be a different kind of walk.

It was a perfect day for hiking: midsummer, but warm, not hot. Overhead, small scattered puffs of white floated on a vast sea of blue.

I felt less threatened by Lance whenever we were out walking. This was the kind of dog I thought I'd met in Mount Bethel—seemingly problem-free. During our hikes, my dog came as close to normal as he ever would get, connecting with nature in a most doglike way. Lance didn't fit in any-where else. He was neither people nor dog friendly. In the house or around the neighborhood, he could never be trusted. In the woods, however, he appeared the epitome of a well-adjusted canine. Why? Perhaps because he had spent so much of his life outdoors, it provided him a measure of comfort he felt nowhere else. A lot of bad things happened to Lance when he had lived outside in Mount Bethel, but there he was stuck to a run on a property owned by monsters. Now he was outside not by force, but by choice, and no longer being continually subjected to assaults by people and animals. He had more say as to whom or what he would deal with. Things were as they should be in the woods, a world my dog understood. Outside and free, Lance was finally experiencing nature the way he was always meant to.

He bit Clara during a walk on a street in our neighborhood when he had been spooked, but that was the exception that proved the rule. Lance never displayed any inappropriate aggressive tendencies during all the time I spent with him outside in Mount Bethel, while his one visit to our apartment there had been utter chaos. In Canadensis, sharing space with him day in/day out inside a house turned out to be unsettling, to say the least. Meanwhile, outside Lance never threatened me or froze into one of his psychotic trances. I remembered our neighbor John escorting Lance by his collar down the street. I couldn't imagine anyone, myself included, pulling our dog by the collar around the inside of a house. Outdoors, Lance was very much the hunter, but only of wild animals. He showed only a passing interest in the handful of people we ever met on our journeys. In a nutshell, when Lance stepped outside and entered the woods, he went through a metamorphosis—for the better.

We usually walked in forests with unmarked but well-trodden trails. This day was no different. However, as we traveled on, Lance was staying closer to me than usual. When he got ahead of me he lingered, waiting for me to catch up. If I took the lead, he stormed up from behind before there was too much distance between us.

While watching Lance plant his nose on whatever struck his fancy, I thought about the dog we rescued. What a ton of work he turned out to be! The exercise he craved was almost beyond my capacity to provide. However, I was determined to give him all the workouts he could handle, my attempt to, in some small way, offset all those years of inactivity he had suffered. Besides, I used our expeditions to keep my waistline south of the forty-inch mark, so we were doing each other a favor.

When still residing in Mount Bethel, I'd only seen an upside to bringing Lance to Canadensis. Lance was a dog (he had the DNA and teeth to prove it) and ever since I was a kid, I'd been a sucker for dogs. Clara was the same way. No point in trying to explain that feeling. Many will nod their heads in understanding; others won't. Every humane dog owner feels his or her pet is extraordinary and rightly so. Dogs offer that special something to those ready to receive it.

Lance was an older dog but his seniority was never an issue for us. In fact, having found out he was housed in a body described as dilapidated by medical professionals just made him extra special. He shrugged off his physical ailments. Lance's message? Don't let your age or physical condition make you give up on living.

However, after moving to Canadensis, we found we had more than just an older dog on our hands. We had a mentally damaged dog that demanded a saint's patience. We doubted we'd ever be totally comfortable around him in the house, because his best behavior was interspersed with aggressive outbursts. In addition, due to his volatile nature, a relentless effort had to be made to keep him away from everyone else in the world, which, in turn, isolated Clara and me. This wasn't what we had bargained for, yet we still kept him.

Why did we continue living with such a troubled—and troublesome—animal? By the time I met Lance, he had been fighting for his life for more than a decade. When we'd considered having Lance euthanized, Clara and I both knew that neither of us had the heart to proceed. We hadn't rescued Lance just to become his executioners, but rather to add some sweetness to the bitter existence he'd endured for so long.

This dog carried a legacy that was dark and brutal, yet full of courage and resilience. He'd lived a far more tragic life than any dog should, but kept working with what was left of himself. Typically, a dog enduring Lance's kind of life dies at the hands of his owners, other abusers or natural predators, is euthanized, or withers away at the end of a run. By continuing to exist, he was beating all the odds. Clara and I felt compelled to make it a bit easier for Lance to keep beating those odds, even if he didn't always show gratitude for our efforts.

My dog and I were walking side by side now. I knew that would only last until something more interesting caught his attention.

Lance was never a part of the "Do as I say, not as I do" crowd. He taught by example, by deeds not words. For ten long years, he must have either hung on to the dream that things might get better or assumed, quite understandably, that they never would. With or without hope of a better day, he kept seeing it through. Giving up was never on his list of options. After each attack Lance licked his wounds, got back on his feet, and readied himself for the next assault.

Stick it out, even if it seems certain that tough times are going to continue. If you're dealt a bad hand, at least go down fighting. That's the indispensable lesson Lance taught me and he did it without saying a word. A valuable lesson learned is no less valuable because a dog happens to be the teacher. What? Am I calling a *dog* inspirational, a psychotic dog that attacked, no less? Yes. I am unashamedly humbled by this living creature that suffered such nightmarish torture for so long and yet, after it all, was still standing. His bones had been broken, but his will to live had never been destroyed. How could I have given up on a dog that hadn't given up on himself?

I parked myself on a rock lying alongside a small stream. Lance gave a stab at wading, but the water was a bit too shallow for his taste, so he crossed over to the other side and began investigating the foliage.

There was something else, a deeper, more personal and bittersweet part to our connection, having as much to do with me as it did with my dog. A collection of dark memories that I usually managed to keep buried had reared its ugly head, demanding my attention.

I suffered a few nicks and dents as a kid. I learned early on that there was little I could do to guarantee my safety. My sister says she first saw me get hit by my father when I was about four years old. I remember him slamming me against a wall on my fifth birthday. Things went downhill from there.

Quickly growing into a child with an adult-sized chip on my shoulder, I decided that if I could get hit for doing nothing, I might as well get hit for doing something. I became a troublemaker, sometimes hanging out with an older crowd and committing criminal acts. Often I acted alone; Arson, vandalism and shoplifting were my favorites. Some of my actions put lives, including my own, in danger. There were never any fatalities, no thanks to me. Many times I didn't get caught, but many times I did. A parade of policemen, neighbors, store owners, and strangers—all with complaints about me—began showing up at our front door. My father knew exactly what to do after they had left.

Though my young age saved me from legal consequences reserved for adults, at one point, I was placed on juvenile probation. My father constantly threatened to ship me off to what was called a reform school back in those days, telling me that would "whip" me into shape.

During one police visit, my mother burst out crying and I started crying right along with her. Why did I keep hurting her? Why did I keep doing the next wrong thing? None of the law-breaking was enjoyable and it only made my own situation worse.

After getting caught, I'd quarantine myself in my bedroom, sometimes for several days; I was safer keeping out of my father's sight. When my self-imposed exile was over, I'd wear a look of shame for a few days, partly because it was expected of me, partly because I myself felt something was wrong with me, to my core.

The physical hurt I dealt with pales in comparison to what Lance endured. Furthermore, unlike me, he could not emancipate himself at any age. That said, there nevertheless existed a commonality between Lance and me. We both got off to a rough start in life. In Mount Bethel, Lance could not trust his keepers nor do anything to prevent being physically harmed, a situation so like mine as a child. Lance, stuck on his run, must have panicked when any of the Schmidts approached him, just as I instinctively cringed every time my father's car pulled into the driveway. On numerous occasions Lance broke loose and showed up, first at Anna's place and then mine, only to be brought back to his tormentors. As a kid, I ran away from home and, just like Lance's efforts, mine were futile. Lance wasted away for years at the end of a run, while I squandered a large part of my childhood trying to find solace by hiding in the woods. Lance had a negative reputation in Mount Bethel and reinforced it in Canadensis; growing up I was probably the most despised kid in my neighborhood. After attacking Clara or me, Lance imposed a time out on himself and, after several hours, he'd reappear, keeping his distance and wearing a guilty look. His self-imposed isolation and troubled confusion, brought on by his inappropriate behavior, mirrored mine as a child.

Most of my childhood memories are nothing for me to get nostalgic about. I'm sure Lance felt the same way about his life in Mount Bethel. I'd never want to revisit my childhood, and I'm just as certain that Lance wouldn't have wanted to turn the clock back and be forced to relive his early years.

By my mid-teens, the tables had turned. I now physically dwarfed my father. One day, we almost came to blows. It was time to get out. At age eighteen, I left the house and never looked back. I had escaped the storm, but not its aftermath. I'd developed a distrust and uneasiness around people, especially myself. Love was just another word in the dictionary, one that had no meaning in my life.

From the day I left home, my criminal behavior began to wane. However, I became a loner. Extremely self-conscious and suspicious, I felt inadequate and was constantly on high alert around people, wary of their intentions. I paid a steep price for being so distant. Similarly, by the time Lance finally escaped the Schmidt property, fearing for his life and distrusting people had become a second nature he couldn't escape. I have, at times, lashed out verbally because of my deep-seated defensiveness and resentments; because of his, Lance also attacked with his mouth. If he was bitter and distrustful of people, I certainly understood that. He had grown up an outcast, I a misfit.

I feel cheated. Having lived a twisted childhood, the belief has haunted me my entire life that I am not—and will never be—the "someone" I was born to be. Similarly, Lance was nature's creation, but by the time the Schmidts were through with him, he'd become something nature had never intended. Who's to say Lance didn't feel cheated too?

Some might say I'm comparing myself, a human, to Lance, who was "only" a dog. In fact, a neighbor tried to convince me that a dog, because it's an animal, can't become psychologically damaged by neglect and abuse like a person would, and, therefore, Lance's instability had been born, not beaten, into him. Really? The terms various professionals used to describe Lance were chronically anxious, schizophrenic, phobic, and paranoiac, all conditions suffered by millions of humans and so often brought on by trauma. Thanks to an iron constitution, Lance may have survived the physical abuse, but he didn't escape psychologically unscathed. Did he have residual damage from the life he had lived? You bet. But I do from mine too, so how could I have questioned his?

Was Lance responsible for his bad behavior? Was I for mine as a kid? Let others decide. All I know for sure is that Lance had his blemishes, but so do I. As unnerving as his behavior was, the more I'd lived with Lance, the more I asked myself, *Why would I, of all people, expect him to be any different?* Although man and dog, we were kindred spirits. Kicking Lance to the curb would've been be like kicking myself to the curb.

We were back on the dirt path, heading back home.

As a young boy, I escaped into the deep woods every opportunity I got. As scary as the forest could at times be, I took my chances wandering in it alone, or with my dog, to avoid being trapped in my house. In my adulthood, there would be consequences for having grown up seeking shelter so often in such unhealthy isolation, but at the time, it brought me such precious, if only momentary, refuge. After spending so many years chained to a run and under constant assault, I bet anything Lance experienced a similar rush of freedom and safety that first time I let him loose in the woods years earlier and every time thereafter.

I was giving Lance the long-over-due chance to live a dog's life, but I owed Lance a debt of gratitude, too. He may have had his shortcomings elsewhere, but, thanks to him, out in the woods, I felt like a kid with his dog, enveloped in that same protection nature had provided me so many years ago. Whatever I was doing for this dog, he was doing just as much for me.

Though we grew up fighting on different battlefields, Lance and I were comrades-in-arms. Every time the two of us entered the forest, we gave each other a chance to feel young again. But, unlike years ago, now when a walk ended, I wasn't reluctantly returning to my childhood house of horrors and Lance wasn't getting dumped back onto the Schmidt property to resume his desperate struggle to survive. We both had something to be grateful for.

-41-

Even More Lance-isms

One afternoon, Lance and I were walking by ourselves along a dirt path that bordered a large field. Suddenly, Lance, unprovoked by man or beast, stopped dead in his tracks. My heart sank. Was he having his first psychotic break outside the house? No. Lance's eyes, rather than blank, were riveted on a huge farm tractor with a rototiller, standing in a meadow about fifty yards away from us. At first, Lance, uncertain as to what he was dealing with, skulked and growled. Then, he rushed up to his inanimate adversary and began alternately lunging at and backing off from it, trying to intimidate the alien beast. It was hilarious watching a medium-sized canine attempt to bully a huge bulldozer-sized piece of equipment that towered over him. I had to hand it to my dog. There he was, standing in the shadow of this mammoth metallic monster that had to weigh a ton or more, not yielding an inch. Was he really that brave or only bluffing? I enjoyed the show for a bit. Having had enough fun at his expense, I ended the confrontation by walking over to the tractor and resting my arm on it. Seeing this, Lance cautiously stepped up to his nemesis, gave it a sniff test just to confirm its irrelevance, and moved on to his next adventure.

Among Lance's favorite treats were Greenies™, bone-shaped pieces of chlorophyll. He often buried them outside just as he did real bones. Come to think of it, I rarely saw him eat a Greenie inside the house that had not spent some time outside. Lance wanted his Greenies to acquire that special taste obtained only by letting them fester a while in the soil with its worms, bugs, perhaps a rotting carcass or two, and who knows what else. According to my unofficial count, three times as many Greenies went outside with Lance than ever came back inside. My guess is there are still plenty of them buried around our yard.

Another prize preferred by Lance: Milk-Bones™. I never saw him take any of them outside. No doubt he knew they wouldn't fare well out in the elements. Instead, the ones he didn't immediately consume we found secreted throughout the house in the darkest parts of my recliner, under the sofa or in our shoes.

As earlier mentioned, no matter what goodies we crammed into state-of-the-art, synthetic bones, Lance was not interested. A real bone was a different story. After Lance cleaned the marrow out, Clara picked the bone up—only, of course, when Lance wasn't close by it—and filled it with cheese, peanut butter or some other delicacy. After Lance cleaned out the bone a second time, he'd head outside to give it a proper burial.

Whenever our dog was about to enjoy any of his tidbits in the house, he insisted on having us watch. Maybe he was trying to make up for all those years he had no audience. With the treat in his mouth, he'd wait for us to sit down and focus on him. We could not stand; we had to be seated. Next, he'd drop the goody on the carpet and then begin his ritualistic dance, focusing his eyes on the goody lying in front of him. Occasionally he'd peak out of the corner of his eye to make sure we were paying attention. His dance completed, Lance would go to work on his treat.

Sometimes Lance wagged his tail and wiggled his square-shaped butt while keeping the front half of his body motionless. It looked like his rear end was trying to convince his front end to be happy. Lance happy? I'd like to believe there were times he truly was.

-42-

Lance the Hero

In my capacity as a drug and alcohol counselor at the nearby Monroe County Correctional Center, I met two inmates, John and Lisa Cowan, a husband and wife second-story team. They had been arrested and convicted for committing a string of burglaries in Canadensis, Pa. and were awaiting sentencing.

During a counseling session, Lisa was quite forthcoming in discussing the details of her criminal acts, almost prideful. Maybe that was because the pair had already pleaded guilty and she felt there was no longer a reason to hide anything; maybe it was because she was a sociopath and incapable of feeling any remorse. As we talked, I realized that she and her husband were the pair that had invaded two homes on Oak Tree Drive.

"You know we hit a lot of houses they never pinned on us," Lisa bragged.

"How did you two get involved in committing burglaries on a regular basis?"

"We did them because I wanted to do them. Had to feed the habit [heroin], you know. I did all the work. I was the one who broke the window or busted down the door, because my husband's a wimp. I'm the one who scoped areas for the best houses to rob."

"What would be the best houses?"

Lisa gave it some thought. "Well, for one thing, a house that didn't have a real dog."

"A 'real dog'?"

"Yeah. A real dog like that could give me problems, a damn watchdog kind of dog. I always make it my business to find out what's waiting inside before making a move. I hate dogs anyway. There was only one serious dog on that dead end street (Oak Tree). That house was off-limits. I like soft targets."

Apparently, for Lisa, a real dog was one large enough and protective enough to threaten her well-being. Lance was a very alert dog who, I'd swear, when inside could detect the sound of a leaf hitting the ground outside. (Okay, I exaggerate.) His no-nonsense barking and the "Beware of Dog" sign had to have been a most unwelcome mat to the Cowans, reasons they no doubt decided our house was off-limits. Had they thrown caution to the wind and dared enter, I can picture the kind of reception Lance would have given them.

After getting home that night, I praised Lance. He was quite modest about it all. Honestly, I'm not sure he understood a thing I told him.

Thanks to our dog, I am confident we were spared a home invasion. For once, Lance's cantankerous behavior had paid a dividend.

-43-

Lance the Antihero

It was impossible for me to give Lance more exercise than he could handle. On my work days, I provided him at least two lengthy walks; on my days off, three or four. Even all of that didn't always satisfy his love of exercise. When it didn't, he had no qualms about pestering Clara into supplementing his already hefty workout schedule.

My wife often got on my case about letting our dog in the woods unleashed, insisting that letting him loose anywhere was reckless. She took a leashed Lance on short walks along paved roads. Clara preferred excursions of the non-eventful type. She had been bitten by Lance during one walk. After that, her strolls with Lance proved to be mostly uneventful. However, there were a few...

Our neighbors Dave and Janice Gresham had a huge, shaggy, lovable goofball of a dog, Roscoe. Unlike Lance, Roscoe wanted to be friends with everyone. Unruliness, however, was one thing he had in common with Lance.

One day, after leaving our house, Clara and Lance had walked uphill to the edge of the Gresham's lawn. From the screen door, Roscoe spotted them.

Taking a page out of Lance's book, he broke through the screen and headed straight for Clara and, of course, Lance. Our dog, who had been busying himself among the roadside vegetation, did not yet sense the hurricane headed his way. Clara did a rapid about-face. She yelled, "Let's go home!" and, channeling her inner track star, began running down the hill. Lance, always on the go himself, was no doubt pleasantly surprised by his owner's sudden burst of energy, and more than happy to run along with her.

From behind, Clara heard Janice yell, "Don't worry, he doesn't bite."

Not your dog, but ours sure does.

Would Clara and Lance get back to our house before Roscoe got to them? The race of Clara's life—and Roscoe's, although he didn't know it—was on.

Clara didn't look back for fear Lance would sense something was up. With dog in tow, Clara hastily retraced her way back home, veered into our driveway, and hightailed it passed the open gate, which she quickly closed behind her. None too soon as it turned out, because good old Roscoe had closed to within feet of his target audience. He came up to the fence, tail wagging. Lance greeted him from the other side with a growl that quickly segued into aggressive lunging. Clara had all she could do to contain him. Roscoe didn't pick up on Lance's negative vibes and stood there, still wagging his tail and jumping against the fence. The two of them were trying to get to each other, but for very different reasons.

Janice came huffing and puffing up the driveway, leash in hand. After hooking up Roscoe and heading him down our driveway, she turned around and shouted, "I'm so sorry, Clara." If Roscoe and Lance had met on the road, we all would have been sorry.

There was another time Lance took Clara out for a stroll. Little did he know this walk would be cut short by his own doing.

Clara made a right out of our driveway and proceeded with Lance up one of the hilly sections of Oak Tree Drive. A late 90s Chevy Malibu went flying past them, "too close for comfort" in Clara's words. The car disappeared over the crest of the hill and Clara heard it come to a screeching stop in the distance.

Their walk continued, Lance in his customary investigative role sniffing hither, thither, and yon. They hadn't gone far when our dog abruptly put on the brakes. He turned, stared into the woods that lay between two houses on the north side of Oak Tree and, nose up in the air, began even more feverish sniffing. Then began an ever so subtle growl. After a few moments, the growl was supplanted by all-out barking that no doubt could be heard from one end of Oak Tree Drive to the other. Lance began tugging on his leash so strenuously that Clara had to hold it with both hands and lean backward to act as a counterweight to his forward momentum. Lance was dying to get at whatever he sensed was nearby, hidden in the woods.

As this was going on, out of the corner of her eye Clara spotted the Malibu parked in front of a house further up the road. All four doors of the car opened up simultaneously as someone came running from a neighbor's house. That someone jumped into the Malibu, the doors were slammed shut, the driver did a U-turn and the car sped downhill, again narrowly missing Clara.

Meanwhile, our dog, still barking incessantly, had won the battle with Clara and dragged her to the edge of the woods. Lance was some ten feet into it and busting a gut to go even further.

Clara heard the crunching of dry leaves under the feet of a...? Whatever it was, was coming out of, not going farther into, the woods. Lance continued howling. A rather corpulent police officer, dressed in SWAT gear and heavily armed, emerged out of the forest with a look of utter disgust on his face. Three more officers emerged from separate locations in the woods. One of them was on a phone advising that the perpetrators were on the loose, giving the car description and barking (no pun intended) orders on how to proceed. Clara called Lance back to her and kept him on a short leash. The policemen wisely, and thankfully, kept their distance.

The large officer, apparently in command and obviously exasperated, asked Clara, "Ma'am, where are you going?"

"I'm walking my dog."

"Well, we're conducting official police business. Could you pu-leeze take him home right now?"

A law-abiding citizen, Clara turned around and headed back home to get Lance off the street. Having flushed out his quarry, he had already lost interest in them and was happy to walk off with Clara, happy only because he didn't yet realize his walk was over before it ever really got started. On the return trip, Lance got into a brief barking contest with the police dogs that passed by in two K-9 vehicles.

Apparently, Lance had blown the policemen's cover during an attempted drug bust. Because the intended targets of the sting had been tipped off by our dog's noise-making, what started as a relatively standard police operation ended up as a two-county car chase. Lance's likely infractions: interfering with police work, threatening public officials, obstruction of justice, aiding and abetting a crime, etc. Thankfully, neither Lance nor Clara were ever charged.

Arrests were eventually made and jail time given to the targets of the sting. I never met my neighbor or his cohorts in my capacity as a counselor at the local correctional facility, a meeting that would have been uncomfortable to say the least. Especially since it's quite likely some of the charges they were facing—fleeing and eluding, endangering police officers, various driving infractions—were, in large measure, the result of Lance's loud-mouthed meddling.

This was turning out to be quite the neighborhood. There was the Cowans' burglary spree for starters. We also had a drug dealer living at one end of the street, a mafia legend in his own mind at the other, and half way between them, a pastor running a chop shop. Can't forget the Megan's Law parolee living nearby. Then there was a social worker (no less!) who, in the midst of a long-standing feud with her closest neighbor, set up both elaborate markers delineating her property borders and "No Trespassing" signs, installed a battery of security cameras, and loudly announced she owned several firearms. For added excitement, squatters were sprinkled throughout nearby condemned cabins. So much for full disclosure from realtors.

There's a silver lining to owning an anti-social dog when your home is surrounded by so many anti-social humans.

-44-

Bear-ly Escaping

Then there was that walk Clara never took with Lance.

It was sometime during the fall, early evening and already pitch-black outside. Clara had leashed Lance and opened the side door to exit. Before she could turn on the outside light or her flashlight, he flew down the steps, barking full tilt. Clara couldn't see anything, but Lance could. He tugged so ferociously on the leash Clara had to drop the flashlight so she could try to pull him back to her with both hands. He resisted so she yelled "Pivot!" Lance turned around and came back up the steps.

Clara picked up the flashlight and scanned the backyard. Hello! Just a short distance from her in the yard, two bear cubs were hanging onto a tree, their very large mother standing on the ground nearby. Seeing Clara, mama bear reared up on her hind legs, raised her front legs, and growled—or was it a roar? Then she made a chomping sound with her teeth. This bear meant business. Clara quickly opened the door to get back inside, but Lance refused to retreat. Instead, he put on a show of aggression himself, lunging towards the adult bear and barking fiercely. Lance's strength was such that he forced Clara back down the steps and onto the lawn, pulling her towards the bear. He got to about five feet from mama bear with Clara at the other end of the leash, way too close for comfort. Clara called for Lance to come back to her, but this time he wasn't interested in responding. She tried pulling him towards to the house. No luck. Mama bear now had her sights set directly on Lance.

Clara realized that if she couldn't get Lance back inside, she'd have to let go of the leash and leave Lance outside to fend for himself. She gave it one more shot. She commanded him to pivot and he responded, but in his own manner. Instead of turning around and walking toward her, he edged backwards in her direction, continuing his verbal assault while still facing the bears. Only when he had reached Clara did Lance do an about-face.

Up the steps and back into the house they went. Once there, Clara secured the storm door and turned on the outside light. Lance kept howling while Clara rushed to lock the front door.

The bears continued lounging in the backyard. Having heard that constant loud noise can drive off bears, Clara turned on the TV and CD players at full volume. Only because of the dire situation was she blasting Black Sabbath, a group she utterly detested. Although I'm confident it wasn't music to her ears, she must have realized this was no time for the soothing sounds of her beloved Mozart. She also started banging on a large pot with a soup spoon. Lance pitched in with some of his most energetic canine crooning.

Clara hurried with Lance back to the side entrance, opened the storm door and looked to see if the racket they were making was helping. All three bears were now together on the ground. After giving Clara and Lance, who was still barking full blast, one last look, they ambled away into the darkness.

Clara would not be giving Lance a walk that night. After she called me at work to tell me what had happened, I decided not to walk Lance later that night either.

-45-

Reflections

I was recovering in my recliner. Not after a hard day at work. Rather, it was after an even harder day of walking my dog. Lance was outside, burying his latest Greenie.

I started visualizing gruesome images of Lance fending for himself on the Schmidt property. Never having actually witnessed him being assaulted, these pictures were strictly figments of the darker part of my imagination. I quickly escaped that mental pit, but switched to thinking about the first ten years of his life in broader terms: rejected by his original owners, stuck outside alone every day, dealing in God only knows what way with the heat and cold waves and those fireworks and thunderstorms he so dreaded, to say nothing of the multitude of brutal attacks he suffered. He did not live life, he endured it. Except for Anna's visits, Lance experienced the worst of both worlds: either being assaulted or languishing in abject isolation. Had he perished, his death would have gone unnoticed and Lance unmissed, except by Anna.

Considering the number of bloody encounters he suffered, if Lance had been in the military, he would be the country's most decorated service dog. As it was, Lance's clashes went undocumented and largely unnoticed or ignored, other than by his tormentors. Even though he had defended his life in a war zone, Lance's bravery went unheralded and he was awarded no medals. All he had to show for his exploits were countless battle scars.

To describe Lance's unfortunate condition I coined the term "Schmidt syndrome." Its causes: prolonged exposure to the elements, lack of positive activity, and solitude often broken by interaction of the life-threatening kind. The damage caused by these factors cannot be totally offset by any periodic healthy interaction the dog might experience with any nurturing creature(s). Its major psychological characteristics: unpredictable behavior and mood swings, continual and excessive vigilance, chronic anxiety, phobias, and unprovoked and inexplicable aggressiveness. Its major physical characteristic: a battered body.

It's been said that one learns more from painful experiences than those that are pleasant. If true, Lance surely possessed the wisdom of the ages.

Although still holding out faint hope, deep down I sensed that what Clara and I were doing for Lance was unlikely to ever completely undo the damage done during all those hellish years in Mount Bethel. Dogs, like humans, have memories and, by the time I met him, Lance had to be carrying around a lot of bad ones. The shame was that, because of those first ten years, Lance and I would probably never be totally at ease around each other. The miracle was the bond we shared anyway.

Not Your Typical Dog

DOG	DOG NAMED LANCE
Enjoys doing what bred to do	Stagnant, isolated, and under attack first ten years of life
Lowers blood pressure	I don't think so
Improves your socializing	Made us exiles
Acts as relief during stressful event	Often *was* a stressful event
Raises your self-esteem	How good can you feel about yourself if your own dog bites you?
Undying gratitude	Undying attitude
Mood booster	Emotional rollercoaster ride
Petting calms you	Petting unnerves you
Consistent temperament	Dr. Jekyll/Mr. Hyde
Wants to make friends	Guarded, suspicious, and, at times, downright paranoid.
Loyal	Never certain—could turn on you just like that

Loves enjoyable car rides	Ha! Ha!
Doesn't suffer from hesitation and doubt	Chronically anxious
Gives unconditional love	Who knows? Those psychotic breaks tend to put a real damper on things.
Reliable instincts	Phobias
Doesn't hold grudge	Chip on shoulder
Lots of trust/understanding	Lots of distrust/ misunderstanding
Loved and loving family member	Loved, loving(?) and feared family member
Stable domestic animal	Canine train wreck
Escape from reality	Sometimes all too real
Enjoys being petted and groomed	Pet and groom at your own risk
Get caught up in his enthusiasm	Get caught up in his insanity
Pattern: exercise, eat, sleep	Pattern: exercise, exercise, exercise

-47-

A Dog Like Any Other...

You just finished reading a chapter contrasting Lance with the garden variety of his species. At the risk of confusing matters, I have to be fair to my dog and point out that, in spite of his issues, at times he did indeed act like a typical dog.

He got in the habit of situating himself between the living room and kitchen, with eyes firmly fixed on Clara when she was in the kitchen. She's an excellent cook and Lance quickly figured that out. Of course, Lance being Lance, any food that hit the floor by accident was his and his alone. Only a fool would stick a hand anywhere near Lance when he was eating.

Lance delighted in leaping onto our bed in the morning to wake either or both of us if, in his opinion, we were sleeping too late. When he got older and could no longer jump so well, he'd content himself with pulling the covers off to rouse us.

A simple clucking of my tongue (from our Mount Bethel days) or now also a "pfft" sound out of my mouth—would bring him immediately to my side if he was within hearing range.

Whenever we spent time away from the house, Lance greeted our return like any self-respecting dog would. If left out in the yard during our absence, he'd get up from his sleeping spot under the stoop, stretch, start wagging his tail, and bounce around on all fours. If we went in the house first and then let him in, he'd come charging at us with a face full of sheer happiness, looking to be petted just like a normal dog. In fact, the first few minutes getting reacquainted with Lance were among the most predictable and safest we ever spent with him inside our home.

Sometimes when I was busy on the porcelain throne, my dog would scratch on the bathroom door to be let in. After entering, he'd lie down beside me and patiently wait until I was done with my business. This wait could be for quite some time if I happened to be multitasking, i.e., reading a book, surveying the editorial section of the newspaper, or balancing my checkbook. The man-made scent wafting in the bathroom apparently did not faze him.

Every once in a while, Lance would flop over on his back and roll around as if trying to scratch an itch. I'd always thought this common canine behavior to be a sign of contentment. In Lance's case, maybe it was, or maybe that was just wishful thinking on my part.

Another positive sign? After Lance had been living with us for quite a while, there were a handful of times when, while I was briefly (and, of course, carefully) petting Lance, he draped his front paw over my arm just like a well-adjusted dog would. Of course, despite this apparently friendly gesture, I couldn't let my guard down. Not with Lance.

...or was he?

The morning of February 9, 2006. I was packing, getting ready to go to the airport. Clara's brother Eddie had invited us to spend a couple of days at his Florida home. He was going to take me marlin fishing, something I'd never done. I was going to visit Eddie for a few days and return home so Clara could then go see her brother. That way, one of us would be at home to care for Lance.

Clara answered the phone. It was her sister-in-law, Toni. I could hear her on the other end screaming, "Eddie's gone. Eddie's dead. He died of a heart attack this morning." It came as a total shock. He had finally been getting his life together after fighting a difficult and, of late, successful battle with drug addiction.

I took the phone and helplessly tried to console Toni.

Clara was devastated, as she always had been extremely close to her brother. Sobbing uncontrollably, she collapsed into a recliner and began convulsing in grief. Lance charged over to her and, propping himself up with his hind legs on the floor, put his front legs on her lap. Just like that he was face to face with Clara, studying her intently. You never wanted to be eyeball-to-eyeball with our dog, a flat-out fear-provoking experience, especially for Clara since Lance had bitten her in the face before. She stiffened up, and I sensed something horrible was about to happen. *He's going to attack right while Clara is paralyzed by grief over her brother's death. My God no!*

Before I could even think of how to intervene, Lance began washing away her tears with his tongue. He was showing a gentler side towards her, one we had never imagined existed in him. This was an act of kindness I wouldn't expect from any dog, much less a dog like Lance. Clara turned to me and cried, "Look at what this dog is doing!" I didn't answer. Lance had left me speechless. We both watched in silent amazement.

His mission of mercy completed, Lance got off Clara's lap and lay down alongside her. Now we both cried even more emotionally, not only for the loss of her brother, but for our dog's display of sympathy. I had never seen a dog do anything quite like that before nor have I since. To this day, we both still marvel at such an incredible expression of humaneness, especially since it came from an animal, an animal that himself had been treated so inhumanely.

They hadn't been able to beat *all* the good dog out of Lance.

-48-

Uneasy Riders

A sunny summer's afternoon; another day for another hike. We were walking in local game lands. This was an area Lance and I had traversed many times before. Today I stayed on the trail while my dog did his exploring both on and off it.

At some point in our travels, I heard several motors off in the distance. After a few minutes, the noise stopped. We continued on deeper into the woods. Perhaps a half hour went by and, again, I detected the sound of small engines. This time, however, the sound was getting louder and louder. To be on the safe side, I called Lance away from his research to leash him up. Before I could, the rapidly approaching noise materialized in the form of three ATVs. Seated on them were two adults and a teenager, all of them armed. The adults had rifles; the teen, bow and arrows. I noticed one of the riders had on a T-shirt that featured a derogatory comment about females (First place winner: National Pussy-Eating Contest). He was drinking from a metal flask.

My antennae went up. Here it was the middle of the summer (non-hunting season) and these guys were dressed to the nines in camouflage garb and carrying weapons.

One rider was 30-something with what appeared to be a steroid-aided muscular physique and a taut facial expression—a human powder keg. The teen was gangly and sported the requisite facial acne. The oldest of the three, a middle-aged man with thinning brown hair, a ruddy complexion, and puffy cheeks, who was wearing Air Force sunglasses and an insincere smile, asked me, "What brings you to these parts?"

I tried to keep it light by responding with a chuckle, "My dog, he likes to walk me to death."

"This is a bit off-limits, isn't it?"

"I didn't know that."

"Well, I guess we're here to tell you it is."

The insinuation was: *You're trespassing, jackass! Why? Because we say so.* I considered questioning their legal authority, but then thought better of it.

While this exchange was going on, Lance was doing an all-too-thorough nasal inspection of the three riders and their vehicles. All I could do was pray none of the riders would attempt to pet Lance and set him off. For once, I wasn't so concerned about the damage Lance might inflict on others. I was more concerned about my dog's welfare and mine. If Lance acted up, I didn't picture these people being the understanding types. We were in the middle of nowhere, a nice place to be when on a pleasant hike, but not so nice when in the company of armed wackos. If indeed these guys were crazies, my dog and I made easy targets. I feared that Lance would lose it, and then we'd be cut down in a hail of rifle ammo and arrows. Hopefully, I was jumping to conclusions.

After telling the apparent leader of the pack that my dog and I had walked on this trail many times before without incident, he responded. "I guess you were just lucky up to now."

While this terse and tense (at least for me) conversation went on, Lance had thankfully lost interest in these strangers and was now back to examining the foliage on each side of the trail.

The rider holding the flask spoke up. "We belong to a hunting club and we usually prefer to hunt animals. Ha! Ha!"

Was that supposed to be funny? If so, I didn't get the joke.

The teenager sounded a bit friendlier, but only briefly. "Hey listen, champ. You seem like an okay guy. You live around here?"

"Yes."

"Where?"

His blunt tone made that question sound more like a demand. Under duress, I blurted out, "Over on Upper Seese Hill Road."

Not the best choice of roads. Living there, I would have had to already walk well over five miles just to get to the spot where the four of us were standing. That meant I faced, at the very least, a five mile return trip. Such a distance was by no means beyond Lance's capacity, but that's not your typical walk with a dog. The leader picked up on this and, with an air of suspicion, asked, "And you came all the way over here? What the hell ya doing here?"

"Like I said, my dog really likes to walk for miles."

"Shit, I guess so. You'd think your waist would be a bit slimmer."

All three of them laughed.

The teenager asked, "Hey, listen. Ya ever smoke wacky weed? We got some good stuff."

"I'm sorry. Lung condition. I can't smoke anything."

"Your loss. Man, you've never been wasted?"

"Not in a long, long time."

Nothing good could happen staying there any longer. Of course, the same might be true trying to go. Since neither option was particularly attractive, I conducted a mental coin toss. Decision made. It was time to leave, which unfortunately meant also time to find out if they were going to let me. I called Lance and leashed him up.

"Hey, sorry I intruded. I'll make sure not to trespass in the future."

"I'll say you won't. Ha! Ha!"

"Nice talking with you guys. Take care."

I started walking away, very nervously since it meant turning my back on three very strange characters.

With my very first step, I heard a shout from behind me. "Hey, the quick way towards Seese Hill is to keep going the way you were going before."

I looked back at my three "amigos" and said, "I know but, like I said, this dog loves to walk. I'm going to take the long way home."

I again turned back in the direction my dog and I had been heading and resumed walking. There ensued a dead silence for what seemed an eternity. An overwhelming flood of adrenalin rushed through every vein of my body. Though breathing at a runaway pace, I felt short on oxygen. When all three vehicles started up, I became as nervous as I'd ever been in my life. Not one bone in my body felt safe. I dared not look behind me. Did Lance realize what kind of serious trouble we might be in? I doubt it.

What do I do? Act cool, keep walking on the trail, and risk getting blown away by gunfire *or* make a mad dash for safety into the woods and quite possibly become prey for three lunatics itching to hunt a human?

We had traveled about fifty yards when the ATVs began taking off. Not daring to look back, I instead listened intently, trying to determine which way they were going. To my great relief the sound of the vehicles got fainter. Thank you, God! They were headed in the opposite direction.

What kind of threat, if any, had we faced that day? Although I'm not sure, on the way home I explained to Lance that we wouldn't be hiking in this area any time soon. I also profusely thanked him for keeping his act together long enough for us to get out of there in one piece.

Starting in Mount Bethel and continuing in Canadensis, every once in a while a section of our stomping grounds wound up being deemed hostile territory. Fortunately, we were surrounded by an endless supply of new woods to conquer.

–49–

The Insanity Continues

One day during the summer of 2006, Anna gave us a call. We hadn't heard from her for quite some time. In the interim, she had lost her husband to cancer. He'd suffered a slow decline, and during that period Anna had been preoccupied caring for him. She was nervous about calling, certain by this time that Lance had passed away. I assured her that, although heading for his fifteenth birthday, he was very much alive and not showing any signs of slowing down. I had the sore feet to prove it. She again expressed her happiness that Lance's life had taken such a positive turn. There was a time when she'd given up hope it ever would.

The conversation turned to the Schmidts. They obtained a new dog shortly after Lance's departure from their backyard. Anna described it as a little, "inside" type of dog. Nevertheless, just like Lance, this dog was kept outside on a permanent basis. Lodging was, in Anna's words, "an extremely small enclosure."

It again fell upon Anna to feed and walk the new pooch and clean his living area.

"One time they went on vacation and I assumed they took the dog. This was a chance for me to clean the dog's kennel so I walked down to their house and began tidying. While I'm cleaning up, I hear a dog barking in the basement. I called Louise. She was in Florida. When I asked why her dog was stuck in the basement she said, 'Oh, the dog is right here with me.' I knew she was lying. She got defensive and said, 'Hey listen, we train our dog every day.' I knew that wasn't true either. When she got back home, she called to ask if I would take the dog. I told her I already had a dog, I just wanted her dog to be cared for. I knew she wouldn't have given me the dog anyway. I believe she just wanted me to refuse to take her dog, because that would prove I didn't really care about the dog, so I had no business being in her business."

A few more months passed by and it became obvious to Anna that the dog was left alone in his owners' basement whenever they were away.

She asked if the dog had food when he was left by himself, and Louise replied, "If you are so worried, why don't you adopt him?"

"She knew damn well I was still not in the position of taking the dog in. The comment was made just to make me look insincere in my concern for her dog's well-being."

That dog was run over by a car in New York City, just as Rachel had told me at the ice cream stand. Apparently the only time the Schmidts give a dog any freedom is to let it run in heavy traffic.

Anna continued. "When I called Louise to express my condolences, she accused me of calling her an incompetent pet owner and said, 'Well, I'm getting a new dog.'" Translation: *I'm going to ruin another dog's life and you can't do anything about it.*

Sure enough, the Schmidts now had another dog. Anna said it looked like Toto from the Wizard of Oz. He lived outside (what else?) in a doghouse situated within a sizable steel cage. Anna was taking care of this one, too. The cage itself stayed locked. Anna couldn't feed, clean, or walk the dog without one of the Schmidts opening the cage for her.

Anna questioned Ted, the older son. "Why the lock?"

He replied, "Someone might steal the dog."

Anna asked, "Who would want to do that?"

Ted shot back accusingly, "Well, you stole Lance, didn't you?"

This led me to ask Anna, "What happens if they go away and leave this dog in the basement? Will they leave you a key?"

"Probably not. Knowing the way they are, no, probably not."

"But then if you couldn't get to the dog, what would you do?"

Anna didn't hesitate: "I definitely wouldn't wait for them to come back. I'd call somebody in authority. I wouldn't make that mistake again."

Oddly, even with that insight, Anna was back to being far too diplomatic in her assessment of the Schmidts as pet owners. "They don't do it {mistreat dogs} on purpose. They simply have no idea how to take care of an animal. They just don't know any better."

It was sad. After all these years, the Schmidts still had Anna jumping through hoops, taking full advantage of her concern for animals they could care less about.

Was it really possible Anna didn't know exactly what kind of pet owners the Schmidts were? The way I see it, in a better world, every time the Schmidts bought a dog, it would immediately be stolen from them; in a perfect world, no one would sell them a dog in the first place.

A chilling thought occurred to me. What happens to the Schmidts' latest canine possession if Anna, due to her age, can no longer care for it?

A few weeks after that conversation, we got another phone call from Anna. She wanted us to know Mrs. Schmidt had just entered a nursing home. Although a bit late, was justice served?

-50-

Stream of Consciousness

While living with Lance, the following are a few random thoughts that ran through my mind from time to time:

We keep waiting for Lance to get better. The weeks have turned into months and now years. We're still waiting.

Lance is not responding to our TLC the way we first assumed he would and now can only hope he will. Instead, our caring is morphing into a level of tolerance toward Lance neither of us ever imagined we were capable of.

If I had to do it all over again, would I? Would I have rescued this dog if I had known what a basket case he was?

Lance is teaching me that it is absolutely pointless to expect anything more from a living creature than that creature has the capacity to give.

Some of the situations I've gotten Lance and myself into are inexcusable. There's been a streak of foolhardiness in me since childhood and I can't shake it off. Of course, Lance goes right along with my program—either because he trusts me, or because he's just as crazy as I am, or maybe a little of both.

Since dogs have memories and can dream, are they capable of having nightmares? If so, Lance's must be horrendous.

Lance was a survivor of the Schmidts, and Clara and I are becoming survivors of Lance.

"Whether lounging at home or roughing it in the wild, the Border Collie is a very adaptable dog and can adjust to almost any situation." That's what I read in a book. I don't think the author had Lance's "situation" on the Schmidt property in mind.

Dogs typically don't ask a lot from their owners, but what they do ask for is apparently too much for some owners to give.

There are features in a relationship with a human that you can't have with a dog, but there are also features in a relationship with a dog that you can't have with a human.

A doghouse, a run, and food do not guarantee a dog safety, health, or sanity. Just ask Lance.

Knowing how Lance acts up in a car, how did he fare with the Schmidts when driven to get medical treatment those two times?

For years, I ignored Lance every time I jogged by his doghouse. After meeting him, each time he begged me not to leave after a walk, I did. When he broke off his run to find me, I brought him back to it. How would I have felt if I had shown up at his place one day and found him dead?

I realize that for as long as Lance is in my life, in some sick, warped way, I will also have the Schmidts in my life.

I wonder how many Schmidts live in this country—people who consider a dog their property to do with as they wish?

Maybe the real reason Lance goes after Clara and me has less to do with environment and more to do with heredity. Maybe he was just bad news from birth.

Those first few weeks of his life, running up to his owners, his tail wagging—what kind of response did he get?

The entire experience with Lance defies logic. We have bonded with a dog that is a biter, even of his keepers, and we're not even 100% convinced that he has bonded with us.

I wonder if the Schmidts, when not abusing Lance themselves, enjoyed watching Lance struggle with some other attacker in their backyard.

Lance is doing his best to act like a normal dog. He just can't pull it off consistently.

If Clara had petted Lance right after that time he had gently washed her tears away, there's a good possibility he would have bitten her.

Lance is living longer than the average Border Collie does. If there is a God, did he decide to add a few years to Lance's life to make up for his lost childhood?

Is Lance's predatory nature something he was born with or a warped survival mechanism developed from years of having to defend himself against man and beast?

Just how many other "Lances" are there, dogs who are on track to die prematurely before they ever get rescued?

Sometimes, I find myself feeling resentful when I see other people's dogs living the good life, while Lance got the shaft.

The Schmidts could have tortured Lance to death and suffered no legal consequences whatsoever.

Lance, I bet you wouldn't dare threaten the Schmidts like you do us, and we're the ones trying to help you!

Whoever heard of a dog being so ungrateful? Where's that unconditional acceptance dogs are so famous for?

I wonder if Lance is ever, even for a second, truly at peace with himself. He gives the impression of being stable at times, but maybe he never really is. The fact that his outbursts pop up unprovoked by anything real (at least to us), leads me to think he is dealing with an ever-present illness.

Lance would have been a great dog if he'd grown up in a healthy environment. He was an even greater dog because he hadn't.

I'm living in a house that a dog forced me to buy, and he's not helping with the mortgage payment.

When he's threatening us, we think his instincts aren't working. He's probably just as certain they are.

In Mount Bethel, every time Anna or I corralled Lance when he got loose and brought him back to the Schmidt property, we saved him from becoming a stray, yet condemned him to keep living as a prisoner.

Most dogs are instinctively ready to love the people in their life. Lance lost a dog's blind trust in humans long ago.

How could I have been so oblivious to what was going on in Mount Bethel all those years? How much of a dog lover am I really?

Which is going to come first: Will Lance get better, or will he run out of time? Is he even improving?

At least Lance managed to stay alive long enough to get some of the perks of being a pet.

Dogs are like children—children that grow old but don't grow up. Lance still has some of that in him.

Who knows? Maybe Lance keeps threatening us because he knows he can get away with it. He's testing our love for him. And maybe Lance loves us for putting up with his bites and threats.

Clara swatted Lance on the nose one time out of sheer frustration. That's it as far as corporal punishment goes.

To those who believe in a Master Plan, maybe I was never supposed to know how unstable Lance was until after I took him in.

Funny how things work out. Lance was an abused dog; I had my issues growing up; Clara, one of seven siblings, was targeted by her mother for "special" treatment; Winky had been a stray. We were four survivors living under the same roof.

If we had put down Lance, he would have suffered the ultimate punishment for someone else's crime.

According to Lama Surya Das, "Dogs teach us about faith, trust, and devotion; how to never give up; and how to keep coming back and just show up... which is more than half the battle." Throughout his life, Lance has never given up and has always kept coming back and showing up. In that, he set an example. But because of the kind of dog Lance is, Clara and I not only have to never give up, keep coming back, and showing up, but also need to have faith, trust, and devotion in order to handle the task of living with him: faith that there is a purpose to what we are doing, trust that this dog appreciates our efforts, and devotion to a task that so often feels thankless. Maybe we are teaching Lance a thing or two.

-51-

Too Close for Comfort

After taking thousands of journeys with Lance into the deepest bowels of the nearby forests, I'd never encountered a bear. Clara already had two close encounters with them without even leaving our property. I envied her. Why? Let's call it my senseless sense of adventure.

A day in late spring, early evening around six o'clock. Our last walk of the day. For that I was undoubtedly a lot more grateful than Lance.

Upon entering the woods opposite my home, I unleashed Lance, and he began to roam about, only a few yards in front of me.

Minutes into our walk, I spotted something on the horizon that brought me to a standstill. Not much more than fifty yards ahead, due east of us, lumbered a mama bear with her two baby bears, silhouetted by the still bright sun and crystal clear blue sky. They were walking single file headed from my right to my left. What an awesome scene. I wasn't watching a National Geographic television program—I was in one.

My feeling of wonder was quickly dispelled by the realization that a potential disaster lay in waiting. Fortunately, the bears had not yet sensed our presence. Fortunately too, Lance was not yet aware of them. If he got wind of their whereabouts, would he use his head as he had that time he chased off a bear from the relative safety of our deck, or would he be his more typical daredevil self, the one that had almost dragged Clara along with him into a fight with a bear and her cubs in our backyard? Which Lance was with me today? I couldn't think of one good reason to stick around and find out.

Although the animals appeared to be heading away from us, I was certainly not going any deeper into those particular woods at that particular moment. Funny—now that bears were standing right in front of me, the prospect of the encounter getting any closer had little appeal. My sense of adventure did have limits, after all!

For the moment, Lance was still totally engrossed in his immediate surroundings. That wouldn't be the case for long. His back facing the bears, he was standing even closer to them than I was. In a matter of seconds, they would show up on his radar, he'd make a ruckus, and all hell would break loose. This was exactly the kind of situation Clara had in mind when she lectured me about entering the woods with Lance. I used to argue the point with her. "What could be more dangerous than you letting that crazy dog take food from your mouth?" Today, I had my answer.

Mama bear turned in our direction. Her head went up and she began sniffing. *Why, I do believe she's spotted us!*

I calculated two distances, the one between mama bear and me, and the one between me and my house. They were about fifty and one hundred yards, respectively. *How fast can bears run?* For some reason, forty miles an hour came to mind. If I broke into a run before the bear did, I might make it back home; so might Lance, if he had the sense to. *What if he didn't? Would I take off and let him fend for himself, or would I stay with him and try to drive the bears away? Did I have the guts to do that?*

At least for the moment, mama bear was looking at us only in curiosity. Since she wasn't running yet, neither would I.

Lance yanked his head up and began excitedly sniffing the air. I had to act quickly. Fortunately, Lance had long ago learned the command "Pivot—let's go!" I gave it and that's what he did, turning around and coming back to me. Quickly leashing him, we turned to head back to the house. All I could do was pray that Lance wouldn't get wind of what was standing behind him just yards away. The last thing I wanted was to be in a tug of war with the devil dog if he spotted his "prey."

There's an old saying: "Never look behind you. Something might be gaining on you." My curiosity, mixed with fear, got the best of me. Taking one look back—one was enough—I saw that the bear, although watching us intently, was not moving. She seemed to be weighing her options. I was grateful for her indecision.

On the way back home, there was no stopping to smell the roses or anything else. Trust me when I tell you, we made the return trip to the house in record time.

Lance, probably disappointed by such a short trek, would never know what didn't hit him. Thankfully, this all occurred within a short distance from my house. Had we all met in the forest's depths...who knows?

Unlike the adventures with bears Lance had experienced with Clara, the most exciting thing about today's unusually short walk was not what happened, but rather, what didn't.

-52-

"Border" Patrol

TRYING TO CONFINE A BORDER COLLIE CAN BE AN EXERCISE IN FUTILITY.

– BORDER COLLIE RESCUE ASSOCIATION

Lance was a bolter, whether from the house door, fence gate, the car, or anything else that cramped his free spirit. He didn't simply exit. He took off as if someone had yelled "Fire!"

He was also a leaper. In our Mount Bethel days, I got him to jump in the air for treats. I'd hold the treat ever higher and Lance would meet the challenge. Eventually, Lance and I were on eye level as he grabbed his tasty reward. The damage both his hind legs had suffered made his leaping ability that much more remarkable. As earlier mentioned, when we were having a large portion of our property fenced, the salesman from the company doing the work recommended adding an additional foot of height—five feet high in all—just to be on the safe side.

One day, months before we had the fence installed, our dog combined his bolting and leaping talents into a particularly unique demonstration. Lance was out on the porch, making himself comfortable on a sofa-sized glider. Spotting a deer on the lawn, Lance decided to give pursuit. He would have to break through screen mesh to do it. He did. He took a flying leap through the mesh and landed on the lawn ten feet below from where he began his flight. By the time he hit the ground, the deer had vanished into the woods. Ignoring my calls, Lance also disappeared into the woods. More than an hour passed before he returned from his unscheduled hike. To prevent further such escapes we installed four-foot-high wood latticing around the entire inside of the porch. We also set up obstacles to keep him off any furniture he might try to use as a launching pad.

The next time we let him out onto the porch, Lance sized up the new layout, and, no doubt disappointed, hit the floor and did his best imitation of a normal dog at rest. We had successfully Lance-proofed the porch.

In addition to the above-mentioned skills, our dog was a runner extraordinaire. In the wide-open woods, Lance seldom walked, he darted. The world was not big enough to hold Lance; he was always pushing its boundaries. Perhaps because he had been confined to one minuscule spot for so many years, he was now trying extra hard to make up for all the exploring he had missed out on.

Armed with all of the above information, I probably shouldn't have been so surprised on that early fall afternoon when a police officer showed up at our front door.

Okay...what now?

Before I let the officer in, Clara let a barking Lance out into the backyard. She went along, making a fruitless attempt to quiet him. Quickly realizing the futility of it all, she came back inside, leaving our dog outside. A conversation ensued, with Lance's yapping as background music.

"Folks, I'm Officer Karol. Barrett Police. We've gotten a report that a loose dog was waiting with the kids at the bus stop down at the end of your street."

Hearing this immediately conjured up visions of bloodshed soon to be followed by a flood of lawsuits. A conversation I wanted no part of continued.

"Your dog fits the description of the dog in question. In fact, the caller was sure it was yours."

"What day was that?"

"Today."

"Officer, we usually let him outside early in the morning to do his business. He stays out for a while, but our yard is fully fenced. We both make a habit of checking the gate before he goes out." I didn't add that we did that because of his biting tendencies. No need to provide too much information, information the policeman probably already had anyway.

"Well, you'd better check for holes. Plenty of dogs are diggers." He was right about that. Lance by this time had buried bones and Greenies by the dozens. On other occasions, with nothing to bury, he spontaneously and feverishly dug holes, just for practice. Thanks to Lance, our backyard looked like a minefield.

Fearful of the answer, I nevertheless asked, "What was he doing at the bus stop?"

"Oh, just hanging out with the kids. Apparently, he wasn't seriously bothering anyone, but I guess your dog has a reputation."

That got no answer from me, but did elicit another question.

"Did he threaten anyone?"

"Like I said, we didn't get any reports like that. You just can't let him run loose."

After a brief pause, Officer Karol, smiling ever so faintly, said, "Actually, there was something kind of funny. Your dog must've mixed in with the kids and somehow wound up on the bus. I guess the kids warned the driver about him so he played it safe and threw half his lunch out the bus to get him off. But when the bus left, the dog chased after it. You know, (Route) 447 is a dangerous road for a dog to be running loose on. The dog catches up to the bus at one of its stops. He starts circling in front of it—just wouldn't get out of the way, like he didn't want to let it move. The driver has to get out of the bus and lead the dog over to the woods and chuck the rest of his lunch into it. Meanwhile, traffic is building up because of the stopped bus. He flies back to the bus and takes off. He didn't see the dog on the rest of his route. *[Must've been a pretty good lunch. Lance would usually rather run than eat.]* Like I said, you're lucky your dog made it all the way back here in one piece."

To reassure myself, I asked a question disguised as a statement of fact: "He didn't bite anybody."

"No reports."

Thank you, dear Lord! I'm going to have another serious talk with that dog.

In truth, I was beginning to question the value of all the conversations he and I had. I'd read somewhere that the Border Collie is quite the freethinker. There were times Lance did his own thing, and I wasn't sure if he was unable to understand my English or just tuning me out. Even when he appeared obedient, was he really, or did it just so happen that my wishes coincided with his?

"Okay, officer. I'll check the yard right away. That devil probably dug a hole way in the back. I guess I'll have to walk the property on a regular basis."

"I would if I were you. If I have to come back, there'll probably be fines. If he bites people, well you know, at some point you could lose your dog, if he's as dangerous as they say. You've gotta do a better job of confining him."

On that happy note, Officer Karol headed for the door. The procedure was reversed; I let the officer out the front door before Clara let Lance back in via the side door. Once inside, Lance feverishly smelled down the general area where the policeman had been standing.

"Lance, what the hell have you been up to?"

Not surprisingly, my question didn't elicit an answer. Magicians don't like to give away their trade secrets.

I had long ago stopped letting Lance run unleashed on the streets. We had also installed a fence to prevent our dog from wandering. Apparently, he was making a mockery of our efforts to contain him.

Outside I went, to do a painstaking survey of the entire perimeter of the chain-link fence. Lance was more than happy to join me on my inspection of the yard, merrily wagging his tail throughout the tour. I suspected he found it all very entertaining, that he was reveling in the fact he could escape from the yard right under our noses. If it's at all possible for a dog to do, Lance had to be laughing to himself. I, on the other hand, wasn't. Escaping and running loose, police, the bites and fines that would inevitably follow—I failed to see the humor. The whole thing was aggravating and more than a bit embarrassing. No way was I going to let this four-legged Houdini keep making a fool of me.

My inspection revealed nothing. Along the fence there wasn't one sign of a dog's digging, or anyone else's for that matter. I checked the gate; it was closed and all was in working order.

I didn't get it. What was going on? No neighbor in his or her right mind, no matter how badly wanting Lance to run off and never be seen again, would have dared open our gate and willingly risked an encounter with him.

Because of Lance's temperament we made an extra effort to monitor his whereabouts. There wasn't any way Clara or I would have left the gate open, or was there? Even if we had accidently left it open and he had gone out and come back, I couldn't picture him closing the gate behind himself after returning. Or, upon getting back home, did he leave it ajar and Clara and I simply hadn't noticed?

Lance certainly couldn't open the gate, or could he? I thought back to that incident when Clara and he were dealing with a bear on our property and Lance had magically appeared on the front deck. We never figured out exactly how he had gotten out a closed front door, but he had.

What if the gate had neither been left ajar nor opened by our dog? I tried to picture Lance, with a running start, jumping and clearing the fence. A five-foot fence? That old coot? The idea of him clearing it—or climbing over it—seemed preposterous. On the other hand, this dog specialized in the preposterous.

Whatever the case, I wasn't taking any chances. I secured the gate with a heavy-duty bungee cord. That way, even if Lance lifted up the latch, he would still not be able to squeeze through the gate. If he was jumping the fence, that would be a whole other matter. I'd have to get a higher one. If he was climbing over it, maybe an even higher one. Lance was becoming a fence salesman's dream.

I went back inside and we counted our blessings. Lance, on the loose around a bunch of children, had not attacked anyone. Did he have a soft spot for kids? I wouldn't bet on it.

I found the whole thing baffling.

Baffling, that is, until one day several months later. Every so often, deciding to be proactive, I'd invite Lance to take a walk just to avoid his pestering me for one. Some kind of preemptive strike on my part but, of course, Lance was still getting what he wanted anyway. This particular day he was out in the yard so, grabbing the leash, I headed for the side door. Through the door window I saw something that stopped me in my tracks.

What did I see? Why, it was Lance, caught in the act, standing on his hind legs and balancing himself on the fence with his front legs, while nudging the gate latch with his snout. Instead of stopping him, I found myself watching in frozen fascination. Several nudges got him nowhere and then, that son of a gun got the latch up and off. He began pushing on the gate with a front paw. Thanks to the bungee cord, he was frustrated in his attempts to escape. Lance wasn't going anywhere, but he didn't know it just yet. Propped up on his hind legs, he started slamming both front paws against the fence. That, too, got him nowhere. Realizing he couldn't open the gate, Lance stopped trying to and took a stance on all fours, staring at the fence. I was watching a dog deep in thought, weighing his options. He wasn't ready to quit. No doubt he was deciding what to do next: try to jump the damn thing or scale it. Although tempted to wait and see what his brain would cook up, I decided against it. I yelled to Lance that we were going for a walk. That got his attention.

Daddy's going to let me run. Why knock myself out?

He came charging at me to get leashed and, in minutes, was in the woods, free as a bird.

Now I knew who had opened the gate on that school day months ago. One mystery was solved. Who or what had closed it when he came back home remains a puzzle.

That bungee cord certainly wouldn't be coming off the fence anytime soon. I'd read in a book that a Border Collie never gets tired of trying out new strategies to overcome what he considers a challenge. It occurred to me: *Could he possibly undo or destroy the bungee cord itself? Or, if I padlocked the gate, would Lance figure out how to pick the lock?* If you're laughing that's because you've never lived with a Border Collie. Or maybe because you have.

I no longer had the luxury of assuming Lance would stay put. After all, this was a dog that had constantly gotten loose from his run in Mount Bethel, sometimes by sheer strength, other times in ways still unknown. As noted above, at our current residence he got past a closed door and onto the deck to drive off a bear. Then, thanks to Officer Karol we found out he had left the yard unbeknownst to us. I had the strongest suspicion that wasn't the first time he had gone AWOL from our property. If my assumption was correct, I shuddered to think what kind of nonsense he might have gotten into during his other unauthorized excursions. I would have to start keeping a closer eye on Lance when he was out in the yard, chain-link fence and all. Mental memo: *If he gets loose one more time even though the gate is secured—call the fence company!* There's never been a moment's rest with this dog.

I certainly wasn't about to congratulate Lance for any of his disappearing acts. At the same time, I had to admit being impressed by his uncanny ability to not let doors, fences, screen windows, leashes, or leads stymie his wanderlust. After all, unlike a professionally trained television or Hollywood stunt dog, Lance was a *self-taught* escape artist.

–53–

Catch and Release

A RESCUED OR SHELTER DOG IS MORE THAN HIS PAST EXPERIENCES. HE IS A MARVELOUS INDIVIDUAL COMBINATION OF GENES, PERSONALITY TRAITS, NERVE, HUMOR AND MOST OF ALL, POTENTIAL. THOSE WHO SEE HIM AS A VICTIM MAKE HIM ONE.

– JULIA V. MCDONOUGH
FORTUNATEK9.COM

Oh no! He's badgering me for yet another walk. Isn't he getting a little old for this? I know I am. I see by the clock on the wall it's 4:15 p.m. Lance is ahead of his own demanding schedule. I've already endured three expeditions today, but that doesn't matter to the devil dog. Resistance is useless! Off we go.

I took Lance down to the nearby field where horses were kept and let him loose, hoping he would be content hanging out with his equine buddies, as he sometimes was. No such luck. Today Lance paid scant attention to the horses. Instead he sprinted for the far side of the field where lay the beginning of a path that led deep into a forest. Reluctantly I followed, knowing that whenever we set foot on this trail a grueling hike followed. Today would be no exception.

Within moments of entering the woods, we were magically transported into another world—one of serenity and natural beauty. While I began soaking in the ambience, my dog went about his business.

Lance, even by his own standards, was especially active, conducting one of his most exhaustive investigations. Darting from one side of the path to the other, he seemed unable to keep his focus on any single object very long, before another farther down the trail grabbed his attention. Can a dog have ADHD (Attention Deficit Hyperactivity Disorder)? Since Lance was way too busy to discuss the matter, I took the liberty of making that diagnosis based on visual evidence.

I resigned myself to just keep walking. After all, that was my job on these excursions. Did Lance assume I was having as much fun as he was? Did he ever think it odd that I didn't get down on all fours and sniff this or that like he did, or break into sprints like his?

While Lance did his thing, I dutifully plodded along with him. I kept telling myself, *This is a recording. I am enjoying myself. He's keeping me in shape. He's keeping me in shape. I am enjoying myself. This is a recording.*

As we walked on, thoughts of fatigue gradually evaporated and my attention surrendered to the calming atmosphere surrounding me. Nature was distracting me in a most pleasant way. Early summer and sunny, all the trees in full bloom and the ground foliage about as thick as it could get. Different birds were singing different songs, yet somehow they were in harmony with each other. From the sound of this joyous noise, it was clear these feathered creatures were as happy as Lance to be part of nature's realm. A sporadic breeze caused leaves to flutter, providing accompaniment to the birds' cheerful music. The relaxing sound of a fast-flowing stream that paralleled the path completed nature's version of a symphony. I got lost in it—the symphony, not the woods.

We traveled on.

Eventually, reality, in the form of my literally dog-tired legs, interrupted my nature-induced reverie. I decided we had reached the turnaround point in this walk and did an about-face, comforting myself in the knowledge that every subsequent step would no longer be away from home, but toward it.

Lance had other ideas. He stuck his head up in the air and started sniffing feverishly. He became agitated and jumpy, like a runner at the starting line. I recognized the body language. He was ready to take off. He gave me a look that said *Follow me!* No way. I had fallen for that trap before and always came out the worse for wear—cuts, scrapes, bruises, loaded with briars from head to toe, etc. Not today, thank you! Lance, of course, didn't worry about such things. Into the brush he went. I stood there, expecting him to reappear in short order. He didn't.

I resumed my journey back home, figuring my dog would eventually burst out from the bushes somewhere along the trail. This figuring was broken by the sound of barking. Next, I heard rustling in the woods. Then, it sounded like running. Was Lance chasing or being chased by something? I couldn't picture anything he would run from, so I guessed he had taken off after something (please, at least be something and not *someone!*). Suddenly, dead silence, except for nature's continuing background music. Walking back to the spot where Lance had left the path, I debated entering the woods myself. Not wanting to wade through the brush in an aimless search, I decided to wait there and let Lance work his way back to me. I waited and waited and waited some more.

Finally, I spotted Lance way down the trail, a distant black-and-white speck heading toward me. As he neared, I realized he had something in his mouth. Once he got even closer, I recognized what had been snatched by Lance's jaws of death— a rabbit, and a very young one at that. I was relieved to see that his prey, scared to death to be in a dog's clutches, was still alive and apparently unharmed. The rabbit's heart was beating furiously, his face signaling sheer panic.

Lance stood in front of me, deciding what to do with his victim, while I decided what to do with Lance. There was no way I was going to try prying his mouth open. Instead, I gave the command "Drop!" Although not sure that was something we'd ever taught him, what else could I do? Upon hearing my order Lance looked at me quizzically, still holding on to his quarry. Had he intended to finish the rabbit off and give it to me as a prize? If so, it was a prize I didn't want. I said "Drop!" a second time. Not letting go, Lance instead adjusted his grip on the rabbit dangling from his mouth.

The three of us were suspended in time, with two of us deciding on the fate of the third. Lance stared at me, trying to make sense of my command. *He wants me to let go of it? How could Daddy turn down my hard-earned gift for him? If I let this animal go and Dad suddenly decides he wants it, I'm not going to try to track down this prize a second time. It doesn't make sense to me, but he's my Dad so I guess I should do what he wants me to.* Lance let the rabbit loose. Off it sped, literally running for its life. If Lance considered the rabbit a gift, I had rejected his offering without providing an explanation. I praised my dog, but I'm not sure he knew why.

Enough walking and excitement for one day. We headed back home. On the way, I sorted out what had just happened. Lance had put on quite a performance; it was something special. First, as an aging, but still crafty hunter, he had managed to catch an animal that was younger, more agile and possibly faster than he. Then, Lance figured out what I, the human, wanted him to do, based on a one-word command he'd most likely heard for the first time in his life. Finally, he put his owner's wants ahead of his own strong predatory instincts. This dog that had killed, and sometimes eaten, larger prey, let the rabbit go.

What an impressive display of intelligence, self-discipline, and obedience. Considering this was the work of a dog with such a violent history, it was more than just impressive—it was incredible.

-54-

(Good to) The Last Bite

Autumn of 2007. Early evening. Lance and I had just finished one of our customary hikes, this one in the pouring rain. Arriving home soaked, we both went to the living room to dry out, aided by a crackling fireplace. As I settled into a recliner, my dog came over and stood alongside me. While absentmindedly patting Lance's rump, he whirled around and bit my hand. I'd let my guard down and paid the price.

Clara, unaware of what had happened, walked into the living room just as Lance banished himself to the bedroom. I concealed my wound with a newspaper, not wanting her to know what had happened. Like me, she always kept clinging to the hope that our dog was on the mental mend. No need to disappoint her.

At the first opportunity, I went into the bathroom and checked out the damage. Lance had torn the skin of my hand in two places, drawing blood from me for the first time.

Physically, this event was hardly of consequence. Emotionally, it was very discouraging. From the day we took him in, I had set the bar very high: no matter how often Lance growled at me or tried to bite me, I told myself ours was a normal owner/pet relationship as long as he didn't actually draw blood. That fantasy was now out the window.

I finally threw in the towel and canceled my subscription to Lance's mental recovery. He was never going to become a fully functional dog, so I was no longer going to hold my breath waiting for that to happen. I finally faced the fact that when I met Lance, it was already way too late; his fate had been sealed many years earlier. It had been awhile since Lance threatened either of us, but every time he appeared to have finally straightened out, there'd be another incident like tonight's. After all these years, Lance was back at square one; it was doubtful he'd ever left it to begin with. More likely, Clara and I had created the illusion he was improving by becoming more proficient at not agitating him.

Was I a friend or an enemy in Lance's eyes? Was I both? That's the question I'd been asking myself for years and I was no closer to an answer. Were we fools for making so many sacrifices, for an animal no less!? *This dog is nothing but an endurance contest. Here we are doing a good deed all these years and this is how he repays us? Ungrateful mutt!* Then something else occurred to me. *Maybe the ultimate good deed is one that is done with nothing expected in return.*

Owing her the truth, a few days later, I told Clara what had happened. We accepted this setback just as we had accepted all the others. This time, however, we both stopped holding out hope that, given enough time in the right environment, Lance would be able to overcome his past. We could treat the symptoms, but never cure the disease. There were a lot of things right about Lance, but there would always be something wrong with him.

This incident ushered in a new era. During subsequent attacks, it became a bit easier to evade my dog's snarling mouth. Any rekindling of hope that he had suddenly and at long last gotten mellower was quickly doused by the more realistic conclusion that he was simply getting older and slower on the draw and that, following that bite, I had made myself even more adept at sensing his impending strike.

On a lighter note: (1) I no longer bragged to Clara about my lightning-quick reflexes. (2) Following that incident, whenever I worked up the courage to give Lance a brief, friendly pat, I was literally petting "the hair of the dog that bit me."

–55–

Nowhere to be Found

Midwinter. Lance and I were on one of our epic treks within the Delaware State Forest. When we began our sojourn it was about 4:00 p.m. and still light out. That was hours ago.

We had already put in a lot of mileage on this walk. Having been trained and conditioned by Lance for so many years, I now often hiked without resting just as he did. No doubt, that was one of the things Lance liked about me.

Ignoring the fact that it was getting later and darker, I decided to go off the well-traveled path. These extra-long hikes were rarely planned; they just spontaneously materialized. Lance was more than happy to follow me.

We continued to travel farther away from the known and deeper into the unknown. As the sun set, the now unfamiliar territory gradually took on a hostile aura. The sky became darker, the visibility poorer, and I more disoriented. To further complicate things, I had brought along neither a flashlight nor a cell phone, having made the assumption we would be back home in a timely fashion. The reality was that time, Lance, and I had together marched on.

A cold winter's afternoon eventually segued into an even colder winter's night. The temperature had been dropping all day and was now in the single digits. A howling wind added to my growing discomfort. To top it off, for the occasion I was wearing only sweatpants, T-shirt, a windbreaker, and sneakers, not my hiking boots. I had also left the house without gloves or hat.

The only light was coming from above—a brilliant full moon teamed with a starlit sky. Quite an impressive sight, but one I would have gladly traded in for a flashlight.

At some point along the way, I realized I had no idea where we were and, of greater concern, no longer knew the way back home. No matter what direction I chose to walk in, it proved to be a dead end. I sensed that my efforts were only plunging me deeper into a wooded maze I'd never escape. We had walked out of the only world I had ever known and into a darker, more sinister one. This excursion stopped being fun and became a struggle for survival, at least for me. If Lance was so smart, why was he happily tagging along with someone so hopelessly lost? Oh, that's right. *We're talking Border Collie. He's not lost and he's enjoying every minute of this.*

I didn't want to walk anymore, not only because of my increasing fatigue and the freezing weather, but also because I no longer had the slightest idea where we were headed. At one point, a la *Blair Witch Project*, I unintentionally returned to the same spot next to a stream that I had been at fifteen minutes earlier. I was literally walking in circles. The irony struck me that I might be just yards from my house, yet too disoriented to get to it.

Slowly, I turned around in a circle, occasionally pausing to scan the landscape. At each stop, the view was the same: nearby I could make out some trees, bushes, and rocks, all partly darkened by the night, yet also partly illuminated by the moon. A bit farther behind them I was fairly confident lay more trees, bushes, and rocks but nighttime (and my poor vision) made them barely visible from where I was standing. Everything beyond that was so completely hidden by the evening's pitch-black canvas that it might as well not have existed. I'd have been totally swallowed up inside a forbidding darkness if not for the clear, moonlit sky. For that, I thanked my lucky stars, the ones shining brilliantly overhead.

The thought crossed my mind—what about wild animals? Rarely, if ever, had I seen any dangerous predators on our hikes, but I knew I was in the middle of bear territory. Hopefully, they were all deep in the throes of hibernation. There were also coyotes to worry about. My guess was they didn't hibernate.

I couldn't remember ever before feeling so totally cut off from the rest of humanity, let alone fearing I might never see it again. Thankfully, I at least had Lance for companionship. Of course, if it wasn't for him, I wouldn't be out in the freezing cold in the first place.

Desperation sank in. Guessing it was now somewhere around 8:00 p.m., I really was no longer sure of the time at all. I might be stuck in the woods the entire night, having to wait until daybreak when I'd hopefully get my bearings. Since no one was going to find us, we had no choice but to keep walking. On the one hand, I felt too exhausted to continue; on the other lay the fear that by sitting down to rest I'd lose the drive to resume walking and freeze to death right where I was planted. That fear kept me moving, but doubting I could last. Lance would. He had survived worse in Mount Bethel.

Then, it happened. I attempted to cross a stream by stepping from rock to rock so as not to get my feet wet. Some of the small boulders had iced up and I had the misfortune to set foot on one of them. I slipped and fell down into the stream face first, the rest of my body landing painfully on several of the rocks. Although getting soaked by ice cold water, I lie motionless in the stream, fearing a bone or two might have been broken.

Lance came over and sniffed me. Then, he licked the back of my head. Finally, he grabbed my jacket with his teeth and made an attempt to pull me out of the stream. Was he really worried about my well-being or just anxious for us to get back to this walking marathon he was so enjoying? I told him "No! Let go!" and he did. I appreciated his concern (at least he had been yanking the arm of my jacket and not my arm itself!) but I really just wanted to be left alone.

Still lying in the stream, the thought crossed my mind: *Why hasn't Lance, as a self-respecting Border Collie, led me out of this wilderness by now?* I immediately answered my own question: *Because he is having so much fun and doesn't want it to end.* There were two of us in the woods, but only one of us thought we were in trouble. Lance probably felt that at long last we were on an excursion that was up to his demanding standards.

Realizing I'd freeze to death in that icy water, I very slowly and carefully began struggling to my feet. In spite of the pain radiating from various body parts, I was able to stand up and limp onto dry land.

Oh no! My eyeglasses had been dislodged by the fall! Me, legally blind, in the middle of a vast, pitch-black forest.

Back into the stream I went to conduct a fishing expedition. If I didn't find my glasses in one piece, it would be impossible for me to navigate the woods safely in the dark. Soaking wet, I'd be stuck for the entire night out in the freezing cold. That would be the final nail in my coffin.

After some very anxious minutes, I found my spectacles hooked onto a tree root jutting out of the stream. Luckily, they didn't look too worse for wear and I put them back on.

Lost in the Delaware Forest. Subfreezing temperature. Drenched. My hands now so numb I no longer felt the need to keep them warm (I knew that wasn't a good sign). The same woods that had been a welcoming host on all those many hikes now became my own dark, frigid tomb.

Having hours ago lost any entertainment value, this walk-turned-expedition-turned-fight-for-life had me looking death right in the eyeballs. *That damned recklessness of mine. If I become immobile, would Lance wait here with me until we were found? Or would he head home alone? Is there any chance he is lost too? Imagine freezing to death and being just yards from someone's house, even my own. Get a grip. You're not in the wilds of the Rocky Mountains. Only a fool would allow himself to freeze to death in northeast Pennsylvania. But, could I possibly be that fool?*

Time for survival mode. My dire need to keep moving overrode my pain and chills. I started traveling in one continually straight line, letting nothing—trees, rocks, streams, hills, cliffs—force me to change direction. We marched through brambles, slid down slopes, waded through streams (what did it matter? I was already soaked) and did whatever else had to be done to get closer to the prize. What was the prize? Either a house or a paved road would be heaven-sent at this point.

My walking had morphed into gimping. Fearing it was broken or sprained, I favored my left ankle, not wanting to add to the damage.

How was Lance faring through all this? Most likely he was having the time of his life. This was turning out to be the longest hike we'd ever been on. So, for Lance, what's not to like?

The Delaware State Forest is comprised of thousands of acres. Continuing to head in the same direction, I was fairly certain we weren't going in circles or revisiting territory already covered earlier during this hellish hike. Unfortunately, I also had no idea if we were heading toward civilization or only going deeper into the woods. I was either hobbling toward salvation or damnation. My greatest concern was that my pain and freezing, water-soaked body would get the best of me no matter where I was headed.

I visualized Clara at home simultaneously fretting and fuming. Earlier in the day, as I was setting out with Lance, she told me to dress more warmly, but I'd blown off her suggestion. She always questioned my daredevil streak and now I pictured her saying, *"I told you so!"* I swore to myself that in the future I would never embark on another such ill-planned hike, if there were to be a future.

We continued our desperate march. On second thought, it was only desperate for me.

Then, the miracle. I had been using a star-like spot of light as a guide, following it resolutely to prevent any backtracking. The longer

Lance and I walked toward it, the lower and closer the light got. This was no star in the heavens, this was a man-made light right here on earth. We were some fifty yards away from it when I sensed it might be a streetlight. A few seconds later a passing car confirmed my suspicions. We were back in civilization! After leashing Lance, I stumbled out onto the road to get my bearings *(Ow! That damned ankle)*. Exactly where in the world were we? I didn't know, but there was another decision to make. In which direction would we walk on the paved road? I made my choice and proceeded with Lance. Time would tell if I had chosen correctly.

Man and dog forged ahead. At least now we were on pavement. What a relief to no longer be trapped in the woods. If need be I was now in a position to flag down a car and ask for help. But could I really accept a ride? After all, mad dog Lance was with me.

On the medical front, my ankle wasn't getting any better and now my rib cage hurt like hell if I breathed deeply.

Twenty minutes or so later, I saw an intersection up ahead. Pay dirt! We were on Snow Hill Road and the nearby cross road was Route 447, so I knew we were not too far from my house. Reaching the junction, we made a left turn and began the final mile toward home. Although exhausted, freezing, and in physical pain, the fact of knowing that we were no longer wandering aimlessly gave me the energy to push on towards my destination. Plus now I wouldn't have to face the dilemma of being offered a ride and having to decide whether to refuse it or subject some poor driver to Lance's complete lack of decorum as a passenger.

Home had never seemed so welcoming, even if I did have to endure Clara's lecture on my irresponsibility. As it turned out, Lance and I had been gone almost seven hours, most of that time spent lost in the frigid darkness of a menacing wilderness. Clara told me she had been this close to calling 9-1-1. The truth was that there came a point out in the woods when I would have welcomed the sight of search helicopters, my pride notwithstanding.

I cut short Clara's sermon, appealing to her sympathy. My ankle felt sprained, both hands had come this close to frostbite, my knee was bruised, and I winced with each painful surprise attack launched by my ribs. I promised her we would continue the conversation the next day.

After a bowl of piping hot soup, I hit the sack, but there would be no sleep. In bed, the slightest turn set off horrendous pain in my chest. In too much agony to rest, I drove myself to the local hospital in the wee hours of the morning. X-rays confirmed two fractured ribs to go along with a sprained ankle. One positive: despite having been ill protected in the bitter cold for hours, my extremities had suffered no apparent damage.

While I healed, Clara filled in ably, if somewhat reluctantly, as our dog's walking companion, letting a leashed Lance drag her around the neighborhood streets. It took several weeks for my body to fully recover from nature's assault on me.

This impromptu expedition over frozen tundra in the dark of night was one the most physically painful and fear-provoking experiences of my life. The thought occurred to me that I might be getting a little too old for such foolhardiness. Lance, on the other hand, suffered few if any consequences from this adventure, apart from a temporarily diminished walking schedule. Most likely, our walk that winter night instantly became one of my dog's fondest memories.

-56-

Afterthoughts on Nowhere to be Found

Apart from those broken ribs, there was only one other circumstance that kept me from complying with Lance's never-ending demand for exercise.

As mentioned earlier, I developed a physical problem that had first became noticeable in the late nineties. The cartilage in my left hip had begun the process of slow disintegration. In its early stages the deterioration caused only occasional and brief discomfort. As time passed, the pain worsened to the point that I finally surrendered and scheduled to have hip replacement surgery done in March of 2006.

During the last few months prior to surgery, I fell down in agony three times. Two of those episodes occurred at my workplace and were more embarrassing than anything else. The third fall happened while out in the woods with Lance. After picking myself up, I had to take the long walk home virtually on one leg, unable to put any real pressure on the other. After that incident, I modified our itinerary. I'd leave the house with a leashed Lance, walk across Oak Tree to the edge of the woods and from there let Lance loose. While I waited alongside the road, he'd wander into the woods but soon come back where I was standing, beckoning me to follow him into the great unknown. We were a hiking team, and my dog assumed I'd always have as much enthusiasm as he did for going on mammoth treks. Taking long walks had become a physical impossibility for me, but there are some things you just can't explain to a dog.

Gimp and all, I tried to walk Lance as best as I could right up to the day of surgery. Following the procedure, Clara was pressed into service. It took about two months of rehabilitation and recuperation before I was able to again walk my dog in the style he had become accustomed to.

Lance was a stern taskmaster when it came to exercise. He had me hiking to the ends of the earth on a daily basis. The only two breaks I ever took from walking him occurred when I was physically disabled. To his credit, in both situations, Lance showed remarkable forbearance, letting me heal sufficiently before he resumed hounding me for walks. Could he sense when I was convalescing? Could he sense when I was ready and able to again take long hikes? Your guess is as good as mine.

–57–

Mount Minsi or Bust

"Hey, Poopinski, do you wanna to go to Mount Minsi?" He sure did.

This was a sort of anniversary tour. It was January, 2008. Lance and I hadn't been to Mount Minsi since the winter of 2002. I had often thought about taking Lance back to his former stomping grounds, but always quickly moved on to another thought after recalling that fiasco of an attempt years earlier (you remember, Trooper Bevins). Would this be another mission impossible?

Today found me more optimistic. Lance was older now. Might he not also be wiser and a bit saner? Foolish me, of course not. He hadn't gotten more subdued outside an automobile, so why would he have inside it? Guess I had to find out the hard way.

We piled into my car. I was now driving a large-sized sport vehicle so Lance had even more room in which to make a pest of himself if he chose to. He so chose. As soon as the car started moving down the driveway, I knew I was dealing with the same old Lance. For a fleeting moment I considered calling the excursion off. Quickly regaining my lack of common sense, we instead proceeded.

I braced myself for the impending vehicular endurance contest. Lance did not disappoint. He had lost none of his talents as a passenger. I found myself driving most of the way with one hand on the wheel and the other hand fending off the hairy monster I had for a passenger. At times, Lance multitasked: while continually vaulting to the back and then to the front seat, he maintained an almost seamless stream of barking. At other times, if a long line of cars was going by, he sat by a window and got into a rhythmic cadence—one bark per car. Once in a while, and for reasons unknown (at least to me), he gave this or that vehicle an additional bark, at no extra charge.

The huge number of cars on the road forced Lance to scratch pedestrians, telephone poles, street signs, etc., from his hit list. However, as occupied as he was, Lance was kind enough to squeeze me into his busy schedule. Every so often he stopped what he was doing, rushed over to me, and let out a deafening bellow just inches from my ear, as if he was trying to make a point.

Throughout the trip I continued to keep one hand free for fighting off Lance, one hand on the wheel, except when it, too, had to be used to stave him off, and one eye on the lookout for officers of the law. Thankfully, there would be no Trooper Bevins to deal with this go-round. I have little doubt that, if he'd seen Lance in the car, I would have been ticketed as a repeat offender.

Despite Lance's shenanigans, we arrived at the park undamaged. Maybe Lance hadn't changed as a passenger, but once on terra firma I saw a more self-controlled, laid-back dog. No, scratch that. Lance could *never* be called laid–back. But here he was out of the car, unleashed, and I had little fear he would bolt. It was also much easier keeping Lance away from the few people we encountered in the parking lot. Some improvement had been made over the years, after all. I wondered if Lance appreciated his own progress.

As we started out on the trail, the thought struck me: Lance was walking in the very woods where he had been set free years earlier, after having lived as a prisoner of war for more than a decade.

The day itself was perfect: clear, crisp, winterlike in all the right ways. We pretty much had the trail to ourselves this early weekday morning. There wouldn't even be a group of hikers for Lance to herd.

After walking for a while we came to a spot where the trail split in two directions and, ignoring Yogi Berra's helpful (?) advice ("When you come to a fork in the road, take it."), we instead left both beaten paths and headed into the woods. I remembered a spot that featured a huge slab of rock from which one could see the Delaware River. Lance and I had been there a couple of times back in our Mount Bethel days. Today, that was our objective; we reached it in a half hour.

Since nature often goes through its changes slowly, everything looked pretty much as it had six years earlier. I planted myself on the rock and started to soak in the scenery. Lance completed a quick reconnaissance of the immediate area and then sat down next to me. To my surprise, ten or so minutes later he was still seated next to me, abnormal behavior for this canine jumping bean. This was a dog that always wanted to press on and force me along with him. Maybe Lance had reached a point in his life where he could stop and take a little time to savor his surroundings.

Perhaps he was overcome by the significance this particular woods had in his life. Or maybe he was just starting to slow down.

I looked out over the river, continuing my own reverie.

My thoughts were interrupted by a black-and-white snout pushing on my arm. Lance knew I had treats. That, too, was a bit different for him. On walks, he usually showed little interest in treats, even when offered. Now here he was badgering me for one. I was glad to oblige, but didn't give it to him directly. I put it on the surface of the large rock we were sitting on, counting on a floor show. My dog did not disappoint. Maybe he was a bit past his prime, but Lance still put on a fine dancing performance. He actually added a step or two to his usual repertoire. There was only one judge—yours truly—and I gave him a ten.

His dance over and treat consumed, Lance and I took the long walk back to my car. This time, unlike that first ride years ago, he willingly got back in.

No need to describe the ride home in detail. Let's just say Lance was actively involved throughout the process.

It felt good to give my dog the opportunity to visit the site of his emancipation, especially considering what he had gone through before gaining his freedom. I hoped this visit meant as much to him as it did to me.

I assumed we would revisit Mount Minsi during future winters for a few more anniversaries; we wouldn't. Knowing the kind of life he had lived and survived, I always considered Lance indestructible; he wasn't.

-58-

AKA Lance

Confession: Although Lance is the name primarily used throughout these pages, in reality, I rarely addressed my dog by his given name, blurting it out only when Lance had totally exasperated me.

The name Lance never set well with me. Part of the reason was that it just didn't appeal to me as a good name for a dog. It wouldn't be one I'd give any dog of mine. Far more to the point, that name, in my mind, continued to link Lance with his original owners and had a negativity to it. I was certain Lance felt the same way, so I loathed the name on his behalf as well as my own.

In my "dogged" attempt to call him anything but Lance, I often blurted ad-libbed nonsense syllables when addressing him. Clara added a few of her own. Lance didn't seem to mind. He responded to all of them. The following is a partial list of these spontaneously generated nicknames, some phonetically spelled to the best of my abilities. The significance of many of them cannot be logically explained, so I won't even try to. I offer no apologies for any of the following:

- Die-hard (if he hadn't been one, I would never have met him)
- Booby Boobeeka
- Poopinski
- Mr. Poopinski
- Poopinskoleeno
- Boobeeka
- Boobeekadoodle
- Lancie
- Mr. Lancie
- Mama's good boy (Clara's contribution along with the next two)
- Mama
- Mommy
- Boobkadoodle

- Prancie Lancie (for his dancing talent)
- Poopeeka
- Poopinkster
- Boobalinski
- Poopy
- Lanceoleeno
- Watson (after Dr. Watson of Sherlock Holmes fame, for Lance's intensive investigative sniffing activity on walks. I'm referring to the intelligent doctor in the novels. Lance was much more astute than the bumbling character portrayed in the Basil Rathbone movies. This was Clara's favorite.)
- Grover (variation of the typical dog name Rover)
- Mister Poopinkster
- Boobkaleeno
- Poopa
- Poopalator
- Poopy Poopinski
- Mr. Boobeekadoodle
- Mr. Poopeekadoodle
- Mr. Poopeeka
- Devil Dog (self-explanatory)
- Borderline Collie (a play on the psychiatric diagnosis)
- Booba boy
- Poopalinskaleeno
- Mr. Boobeeka
- Mr. Booby Boobeeka
- Dr. Jekyll (when he was)
- Mr. Hyde (when he was)
- Poopeekadoodle
- Poopalinskaleeno
- Underdog (for obvious reasons)
- Woolly bully (naturally!)
- Tiger (as in "tiger by the tail")

-59-

Senior Citizen

The typical Border Collie lives to about age thirteen or fourteen. Lance's boundless energy belied his age and it wasn't until sometime in mid-summer of 2008, when he was heading for his seventeenth birthday, that I first noticed my dog was slowing down. There may have been signs before then, but I had managed to ignore them. I no longer could.

On our walks Lance now stayed a little closer to me instead of wandering off to explore, as if he was conserving energy, something he once would never have done. I began shortening our journeys for his sake. Getting up from a resting position became more and more of a struggle. The day came when he could no longer jump up on our bed and make himself comfortable. Lance had finally begun to show his age.

Denying reality, I told myself he wouldn't die yet, because he couldn't die yet. He had to get his head on straight and live for a while as a full-time normal dog. *He just needed a little more time to get his act together.* That had always been my hope, one I subconsciously never completely let go of, even if it had all the makings of a pipe dream.

One day, while walking towards me in the living room, Lance lost his balance, falling over onto his side. He lay there for several minutes, thrashing his legs and choking. We were beside ourselves, not knowing exactly what was happening or what to do. Then, just like that, he sat back up, slowly got back on his feet and finished his walk to my chair as if nothing had happened. Fighting for his life had long ago become second nature for this dog.

The following day, he lay down in front of me asking to have his belly rubbed. Always a risky proposition, I gave it a shot. As I obliged, he made a halfhearted turn of his head and let out a faint snarl. Apparently he was never going to let go of his unpredictability, but this time he didn't seem to have his heart into being nasty.

By the time 2008 came to a close, Lance still circled my chair when he wanted to go outside, but with less energy and frequency. We no longer took hikes, only strolls. A dog once indefatigable now easily, and literally, became dog-tired. I used to dread the lengthy walks Lance badgered me to take. How badly I wished he could summon up the energy to force me on at least one last monstrous marching marathon.

Walking up steps became an issue. Since this difficulty only kept increasing, Clara fashioned a ramp out of two pieces of plywood and carpeting. We placed it over the four steps leading up to the side door. This ramp was of a width that left just enough space for Clara and me to continue to utilize the steps. Lance would not use the ramp no matter how we coaxed him. He instead squeezed himself into the small space still exposing the steps and continued to hobble up and down them. I'll never be sure if he was intimidated by the ramp or just being stubborn.

In early 2009, I called Dr. Gordon and, after describing Lance's condition, asked him, "Is there anything we can do for him?"

Dr. Gordon responded, "At his age, no. Try to make life as comfortable as you can for him. He's nearing the end."

My voice trembling, I asked a question so painful it made me choke on my own words. "How will we know when it's time for him to be euthanized?"

"Lance will let you know."

Tuning out reality, I tried to convince myself we'd gotten Lance as a puppy, and that, by rights, he should be only seven years old now. That meant he was reaching the end of the beginning, not the beginning of the end. While my concern for Lance's well-being was genuine, it involved some selfishness on my part. I didn't want to have to deal with the pain Lance's death would cause me.

Around this time, one of our neighbors had placed ornamental black metallic images of bears, from two to four feet tall, in his front yard. The first time Lance spotted them, his hair went up and he growled. It took several weeks of passing by that property before he finally ignored the "bears." I wondered if this was typical doggie behavior, or if my dog was losing his edge.

I often work out in my garage. I have a universal gym and an exercise bicycle there. The rest of the garage is loaded with odds and ends. One evening in the spring of 2009, Lance, every day getting less sturdy, came to the opened side door of the garage and spotted me lying on a mat doing sit-ups. He started heading towards me, gingerly climbing over and around all types of obstacles: full garbage bags, weights, hoses, storage boxes, etc., no small feat considering how hobbled by arthritis he was. My guard went up. Which Lance was coming towards me? Too exhausted from doing ab crunches to get up quickly, I lay on my back, ready to accept my fate. I needn't have worried. Upon arrival, Lance gave me a (first and last) slobbering kiss.

With every passing day it got harder and harder to ignore all the signs of Lance's aging. Logic told me it was no longer a question of "if" but only "when," yet all the while I kept bargaining with the Grim Reaper, trying to extend my animal's time on this planet, for my sake as well as his.

-60-
Final Days

As spring gave way to summer, Lance's physical condition worsened ever more rapidly, as if his advanced years—which he had camouflaged so well for so long—had caught up with him overnight. We were watching our dog die.

My walks with him, once measured in miles, were now measured in yards. The roles had been reversed. Now, it was I who had to slow up for Lance. In spite of his increasing frailty, my buddy would never voluntarily end a walk, and I was pushing him to go farther than he should out of some selfish refusal on my part to admit his days were numbered. Clara insisted that I limit his exercise to no more than two ten-minute walks a day. After his exercise Lance, exhausted and panting heavily, would stagger back into the house and plop down on the floor. Though less active with each passing day, he didn't spend much of the daytime sleeping. He'd lie awake on the floor. Often he'd stare at me, pleading for another walk even though he could hardly stand.

Just getting up from a resting position became a monumental task, sadly one we dared not help him with.

Throughout the first ten years of his life, this dog had fought man and beast to stay alive. Now he was battling for his life against an invisible enemy—his own mortality. It was hard watching Lance, the great warrior, become more and more feeble.

In early July 2009, we came home to find our dog in the laundry room, lying in his own urine, unable to get up. He made several unsuccessful attempts to raise himself. Clara slipped a towel under his front legs to assist him back onto his feet. Of course, she had no idea whether Lance would be grateful or snap at her. As if saying *This time I need your help*, he passively accepted Clara's assistance. Once standing, wobbly and disoriented, he had all to do to not fall over again. Lance had told us. *I'm ready to go.*

Clara made a phone call to Dr. Gordon and an appointment was made for a house visit—the final house visit—the following week. The next day, as if to confirm we had made the right decision, Lance fell down while coming out to the porch to join us. Later that same day, I went out into the backyard and dug a deep hole. I had put off that job partly out of laziness and partly because of the grim finality such work signified. Shoveling was tough because the soil was loaded with rocks of all sizes and a thick network of tree and plant roots. Just to make my task that much harder, Lance staggered over to me, lay down nearby, and watched as his grave was being dug. I fought to ignore his presence.

Wednesday, July 15, 2009—a day I'll never forget. I went to work knowing that by sunset Lance would be gone. Later that morning, I got a call from Clara. The vet would be at our house in the early afternoon. On the way home from work, I half thought, half muttered, "It's not fair. You can't go yet. We're not done fixing you."

At home, we sat together in grim silence, waiting for Dr. Gordon. Lance had spent most of the past twenty-four hours lying prostrate on the kitchen floor, occasionally urinating. We offered him food and water, which he refused. All we could do was to clean up around him and try to soothe him with kind words.

Even though the rational part of me knew that Lance had to be put down, I couldn't help but feel that somehow I was betraying him.

Upon arriving, Dr. Gordon suggested I try to secure our dog on the kitchen floor while he approached from behind with the injection. As I held Lance by his collar, the needle entered his rump. Lance whirled his neck around and growled at the vet. The injection complete, the three of us waited, in an uncomfortable silence, for the expected reaction. After several minutes Lance remained conscious and unfazed. He received a second injection. He became groggy, but continued to live. Knowing his life was on the line, Lance made an all-out effort to get back on his feet. He failed. Clara screamed, "I can't take any more of this," and ran out of the house crying.

Lance's restlessness and resistance was making the process complicated. His turning and snapping made it difficult for Dr. Gordon to hit a vein. I put a blanket over Lance's head so that he couldn't anticipate the vet's movements. A third injection was given. I removed the blanket. Lance was still living. Dr. Gordon exclaimed, "I don't understand. I've given him enough to knock out a five-hundred-pound animal." I understood. Lance was being Lance right to the very end.

While holding and comforting Lance, out of the corner of my eye I saw Dr. Gordon shaking his head in disbelief and reaching into his satchel. I guessed he was about to prepare injection number four. I readied the blanket.

Lance made one last desperate effort to get on his feet. I became delusionally hopeful and relaxed my grip, thinking he was going to be successful. *I'm sorry I did this to you. What a stupid idea. You're gonna get up and shake this whole thing off. That's the Lance I know. You always beat the odds.*

He wouldn't this time. Halfway to his goal, Lance began to stagger. He gasped for air and then began shaking violently. He slowly collapsed back onto the floor, laid over on his side, and became motionless. After checking for a pulse, Dr. Gordon pronounced Lance dead. His struggle was over. The die-hard dog had died hard.

As he took his leave, Dr. Gordon said, "I apologize. I'm really sorry for how this dragged out. I've never had...he was a helluva fighter."

Mother Nature and Father Time, with an assist from Dr. Gordon, did to Lance what his abusers had never been able to. A dog that should have died a thousand deaths died once—well past his seventeenth birthday. He had beaten the odds and thwarted all his tormentors.

After Dr. Gordon left, I wrapped Lance, together with a few of his cherished Greenies and Milk-Bones, in his favorite blanket and placed him inside a black construction bag Clara was holding open. I picked him up and headed for the door. All the while, I was sure he was playing possum, that at any moment he would leap out of the bag and snap at me. That's how deeply conditioned I'd become from years of living with Lance. A dog with Post Traumatic Stress Disorder had given it to his owners. Insane as it may sound, at the same time I was afraid he'd lunge at me, I also hoped he would.

Taking him outside, Clara and I walked to the burial site. I lay Lance down into his final resting place. We stood together and paid our respects. Then, I shoveled dirt until it completely covered the bag. Finally, I placed large rocks on top of the soil. Some days later, Clara painted the words "Poopinski—-always in our hearts" on one of the rocks.

On that summer day in 2009, Lance, like all of us do, came to the end of his road. In part, I hadn't wanted him to die before he'd had a chance to experience being a truly content dog. In part, I hadn't wanted him to die because it drove home my own mortality.

Lance had grown old fighting for his life. In his last moments, he was just trying to be what he had always been—a survivor. How else could one explain the epic battle he fought on our kitchen floor?

-61-

A Special Connection

RESCUING A DOG DOESN'T CHANGE THE WORLD BUT IT CHANGES THAT DOG'S WORLD.

(T-SHIRT SLOGAN SEEN AT A DOG RESCUE FAIR)

My childhood had some rough edges to it. In such a situation, a dog can be a real lifesaver. For me, Rex, my German Shepherd, was such a savior, my sidekick and confidante. He didn't criticize me, judge me, or attack me. His moods were predictable. He hadn't been abused. Lance on the other hand, had been. As a volunteer at the local animal shelter, I have learned that there is no single way that all dogs react to maltreatment. Some of the dogs there are dangerous, others extremely fearful, while still others appear fairly well-adjusted. Lance was all of the above. His aggressive outbursts? Whether they were out of fear, anger, or some combination of both, I accepted them. I knew where he was coming from and that made his erratic behavior, although upsetting, tolerable.

As tough as life had been for him right from the very start, Lance stuck it out, his life did get better, and he fought to the end to hold onto it. Does the fact he was dog and not a human make his incredible will to survive any less compelling? Not to me it doesn't.

In some ways, the die-hard lives on. For one thing, Lance coauthored this book with me. For another, he inspired me to do the above-mentioned work at the local shelter, trying to help other "Lances."

Clara and I still experience Lance daily by continuing to live in the house he "bought." There is an eerie peacefulness within its walls that didn't exist for one second while Lance resided with us—call it the calm following a seven-year storm. Even in his absence, we still feel his presence.

There remain constant reminders of this dog everywhere. Every morning I drink my coffee from a personalized mug that features a photo of the devil dog ripping up newspapers. A stained glass painting of Lance, made by one of Clara's coworkers, hangs on a wall in our living room. I have two custom-made T-shirts (featuring Lance's name) that, for emotional reasons, I can hardly bring myself to look at, let alone wear, but I won't part with them either. My Border Collie key chain, although tarnished, remains in use. We also have a collection of photos, some of which are shown in this book.

Outside, the Beware of Dog sign necessitated by Lance still hangs on our chain-link fence, somewhat comically considering that the current canine resident, a twenty-eight pound poodle/beagle mix named Buddy, wants to be friends with everybody. His was a much less dramatic rescue. Clara and I can even pet him without fear of reprisal, which took us some getting used to. No need for the bungee cord on the gate anymore either.

Although my travels with Buddy are not nearly as extensive and taxing as those I took with Lance, we regularly tread over some of the same turf that Lance once walked. Sometimes, I get the feeling he is nearby watching, about to rush out from behind some foliage and join us.

Our current dog also keeps Lance's memory alive in a painful way. The much more normal owner/dog interaction we enjoy with Buddy is in striking contrast to the bizarre relationship Clara and I had with his predecessor. Buddy is the epitome of a relaxed and secure canine. The life he enjoys day in, day out, sits in stark contrast to Lance's bleak existence all those years on the Schmidt property. Buddy expects he'll be treated kindly. When living in Mount Bethel, what kind of expectations did Lance have? No living creature should ever have to deal with the unrelenting isolation, fear, and physical pain Lance did. Throughout his entire life, Lance never fully enjoyed the most vital feature of a healthy dog/owner relationship—unspoken, but understood, total and unconditional mutual trust.

Lance's grave with marker lies at the southern end of our property. Every once in a while I go out there to pay my respects. We ended Lance's life in 2009, but that was better than if we had made the decision to do so years earlier. Given that second chance, he got to take a lot more walks and bury a lot more Greenies.

This dog changed me. All my life I have struggled with a lack of self-confidence that, combined with a tendency to procrastinate and a streak of laziness, has made me a consummate underachiever. As a result, lying in my life's wake are a huge number of unfinished creative projects. From the first day I sat down to begin chronicling Lance's life, I sensed something was different, that this effort would reach completion. Though Lance never got to fulfill his potential, his spirit drives me to do a better job of fulfilling mine. This book is the result of a dog's prodding. Was Lance's story worth telling? The fact that you are reading this page gives me the hope that it was.

I have a daughter that I haven't seen since she was four months old. She didn't find out I existed until reaching her eighteenth birthday. Since then, we have only exchanged letters—no phone calls, no meetings. I don't really know her, but I do know she's a dog lover. I plan to hand-deliver a copy of this book to her. Lance gave me this opportunity; the rest is up to me.

Every Monday on the way to work in New Jersey, I drive over the Delaware River, right past Mount Minsi, home of the park that is the official site of Lance's emancipation. One such Monday during winter a couple of years ago, with many of the trees bare, I "saw" Lance, standing on the side of a mountain, jumping up and down and barking at me. Although he was too far away to hear, instinctively I knew what he was saying: *Hey, forget about work. Come on! Let's go on a five-miler.* A blasting car horn jolted me back into reality. After yanking my vehicle back into the proper lane, I looked to where I'd seen Lance. He'd vanished—rather, he'd never been there; my eyes had played a trick on me. He may be physically gone, but I cling to the hope that somewhere up in those hills his spirit is wandering—completely free.

Call me crazy, but even if it meant having to deal with Lance's fear-provoking behavior once again, I'd take that dog back in an instant, baggage and all. The memories I have of him will be part of me until my time is over.

Thrown outside as a puppy to be forgotten, Lance turned out to be unforgettable.

REST IN PEACE

About the Author

Walter Stoffel is a substance abuse counselor and GED teacher in correctional facilities. When not behind bars, he likes to read, travel, work out and watch bad movies. Major accomplishment: He entered a 26.2 mile marathon following hip replacement surgery and finished—dead last.

The author currently lives with his wife Clara, their dog, Buddy (another rescue), and cat, Winky (yet another rescue).

Contact the author:
walterstoffelauthor@gmail.com

Made in the USA
Columbia, SC
21 January 2018